Under the Rainbow

Catherine Campbell

Isaiah 43:2

Under the Rainbow

A Mother experiences the promises of God in the midst of the storm

Catherine Campbell

AMBASSADOR INTERNATIONAL
Greenville, South Carolina • Belfast, Northern Ireland

UNDER THE RAINBOW
A Mother experiences the promises of God in the midst of the storm

Scripture taken from the New King James Version. Copyright 1979,19
80,1982, by Thomas Nelson, Inc. Used by permission. All rights reserved.

Copyright sought from Gary Valenciano writer of the lyrics 'We are the Reason' (p110).
www.manilagenesis.com

ISBN 978-1-84030-195-3

Ambassador Publications
a division of
Ambassador Productions Ltd.
Providence House
Ardenlee Street,
Belfast,
BT6 8QJ
Northern Ireland
www.ambassador-productions.com

Emerald House
427 Wade Hampton Blvd.
Greenville
SC 29609, USA
www.emeraldhouse.com

Dedicated to:

The memory of
Cheryl and Joy,
who continue to bless my life

Also,
to my husband
Philip
and son
Paul,
whose love and support are my constant strength

And to
Susie,
who is teaching me once more the delights of daughters

With special thanks to:

Mrs. Lillian Hill and the staff of Hillcroft School

and

Dr. E. Hicks and the staff of Paul Ward,
and other departments,
Royal Belfast Hospital for Sick Children

for

your care of Cheryl and Joy down through many years.

May you always remember that you made a difference

***

Also special thanks go to my two wonderful proofreaders:

My husband Philip

and

Mrs. Liz Young,
whose red ink and encouragement never ran out!

And to Ambassador Publications, for taking a risk with this literary novice!

Contents

I AM LEADING MY CHILD TO THE HEAVENLY LAND
I AM GUIDING HER DAY BY DAY
AND I ASK HER NOW, AS I TAKE HER HAND
TO COME HOME BY A RUGGED WAY.
IT'S NOT THE WAY SHE HERSELF WOULD CHOOSE
FOR ITS BEAUTY SHE CANNOT SEE,
BUT SHE KNOWS NOT WHAT HER SOUL WOULD LOSE
IF SHE TROD NOT THAT PATH WITH ME!

(Author unknown)

Prologue

THE changing room was unusually quiet that Sunday afternoon as I arrived for my shift. I glanced at my watch to see if I was late. I wasn't. That meant one of two things, either the hospital wasn't too busy or it was very short - staffed. I hoped the former was true as I headed down to the end of the main corridor where the Sick Baby Unit was housed. Working with the babies was a delight, especially as the unit cared for babies of normal gestation, who usually only needed a few days extra care before they were reunited with their mothers. So much less stressful than working with the very tiny babies of the Premature Baby Unit, whose treatment was critical and intensive.

There was a lilt in my step and a song in my heart as I pushed open the huge door into the unit. Church had been particularly uplifting that morning, and everything in the world was good.

"Nurse, come with me!" brought me sharply to attention. The brusque, even angry, manner of the midwife-in-charge sent my brain into overdrive. Surely I wasn't late? What had I done wrong? The usually pleasant atmosphere was ice cold. No friendly "Hellos" from the other staff who were obviously trying to get on with their own business. Only the occasional cry of a baby broke the silence.

I followed her meekly to a cubicle, right at the back of the ward, which was normally only used for babies with some kind of infectious illness. I had never seen it used during my time in the unit. As we entered there was movement coming from underneath the pink baby blanket. The gasp was out of me before I could stop it, while at the same time the midwife spoke again. "This is Barbara. Born 3 hours ago, weighing 9lb. Apgar score low. As you can see, she was born with gross hydrocephalus and spina bifida. Your job is to look after her until she dies. It shouldn't take long, the surgeons can't help. It's just a matter of time. Her mother won't be visiting, she's too upset. She just wants us to tell her when it's all over." Staccato-like she went on to give me instructions as to how I was to care for this pathetic little specimen of humanity. I could see now why she was cross, and why the unit was already mourning for the living dead. Barbara's head was not just big with the build up of fluid around her brain, it was huge, making her features look crushed and even, dare I say it, ugly. The open lesion on her spine was raw and seeping. The dam of spinal fluid was desperately trying to escape from the open wound, which was now covered by a dressing. Her two paralysed little legs lying limp, as if they didn't belong to the rest of her body.

Instructions over, the midwife looked at me with what seemed like accusation in her eyes: "You're a Christian, aren't you? How can you believe in a God who allows children to be born like that?" It felt like I had been slapped in the face, but I was so glad that she turned and left the room quickly, because, in that instant I could not answer her questions. I just didn't know why.

As I leant over the cot I couldn't stop a tear falling onto Barbara's face. Quickly brushing it off, she rooted, just like any other baby looking for its mother's breast. She stretched, and started to cry. "Feed her," they said. "She'll probably bring it all up again, but the sucking will bring her comfort." Two minutes later Barbara was in my arms sucking away at a bottle for dear life. Where on earth this very sick baby got such a strong suck I don't know, but when she opened her big blue eyes as she finished her feed she stole the heart of this young student midwife. "You are not ugly, Baby, you are beautiful. God put me here with you for this little while so that I could love you until He takes you home," I whispered in her ear. The day was very difficult consisting of a constant round of feeding and cleaning up, and of trying to make Barbara as comfortable as possible. Her heavy head was uncomfortable to hold, but I counted it a privilege to care for her, and as I left at the end of my shift I committed her to God believing she would die overnight.

Philip was waiting outside in the car to take me home. As I belted up, the pain of the day overwhelmed me, and in a gush of emotions and words I poured out my heart to my totally unprepared husband. "Why does God allow babies to be born like Barbara? What had she ever done to deserve it? Surely the midwife was right to be angry with God? She's so bad her own mother can't even bear to look at her! It's just not fair!" Long into the night we tried to understand the theology of suffering. All the usual scripture verses seemed so limp in the light of the baby that I'd held in my arms that day. The fact that God is sovereign, or the truth that "God's ways are not our ways" (Isaiah 55:8) did not easily drop from knowledge to understanding. My heart seemed very far from my head as I tried to sleep.

When I arrived for work the next day I was amazed at the sight of night-staff in the cubicle at the end of the ward. It could only mean one thing - Barbara had made it through the night! For the next five days we were together all of my working hours. In those precious days I would sing to her of Heaven, and tell her of the wonderful Saviour who would be waiting for her. And even if she hadn't a clue what I was talking about, I told her about the glorious new body she would receive. There were times I felt we were visited by Heaven in that room, especially when I rocked her when she was distressed. Peace would descend, and in those moments I knew God loved her, even if I couldn't work out the theology.

My Saturday shift started at noon. "Quick! Hold Barbara while I change her sheet. Her mother has changed her mind and wants to see her, but she's going fast. I hope they make it in time." The midwife put Barbara in my arms, and as I kissed her forehead I knew she really was dying this time. Before the sheet was tucked into the small cot Barbara was in Heaven. So brave. So beautiful. Now so perfect. Unfortunately her mother only ever held her after she had died. When she left, the midwife told me that they never let a baby go to the morgue accompanied only by porters. The last act of care for any baby was for the little one to be carried by a member of the nursing staff. Her tone was now very different to the previous Sunday as she had watched me care for Barbara all week. "I think it's too much to ask of a student midwife," she said, "but it should be for you to decide. I will go if you like." There was no decision to make. It would be my last demonstration of love for this brave little one.

I sat in the passenger seat of the porter's van as we crossed the large hospital site to the morgue. Barbara was all wrapped up in my arms, just as if she was sleeping. There was no conversation. Maybe the porter was a daddy, and this would undoubtedly be the worst job he would have to do that day. The attendant was waiting for us, holding a large door open. "Middle shelf," he said, with no hint of feeling, "take your blanket back with you." "Oh no," I quickly replied, "it is much too cold in there." Neither man responded to the foolish suggestion of the young nurse. Perhaps it didn't sound so foolish after all.

Back in the unit I threw myself into the busyness of my work. My life forever touched by the six day struggle of one little girl. As I settled down to sleep that night I stroked my tummy and said: "Well, little one, at least I know *you* will never be born like Barbara. God will take care of you. Your mummy and daddy love God and He would never let anything bad happen to you. Of that I am sure."

One
Cheryl

"WHAT'S this? Are we going home the long way?" I asked, as we turned left out of the church car park instead of right. "I think it's about time we showed this baby who is boss!" my husband chuckled. "Perhaps a long walk will help this little miss or master make a quicker entrance." Philip is usually much more patient than I am, but now at one week overdue we were both getting tired of people saying: "No sign of that baby yet?" Besides, our own excitement was also hard to contain.

The Antrim Coast Road looked particularly beautiful that night. The sun was still high and the clear blue sky reflected on the still glass-like sea. I was surprised at the number of sailing boats still moving on the water as there didn't appear to be even a breeze. The drive was lovely and the time together seemed somewhat intimate as we shared together the things of our hearts. Soon our lives would change with the arrival of a much longed-for baby. For this little time left we could enjoy each others company undisturbed. We walked far into the forest before an alarming thought hit me: "What if this long walk did have the desired effect, and I went into labour here. How would Philip get me back to the car, never mind the extra miles to the hospital?" I don't know if it was the descending chill in the air, or the slight concern of being in the wrong place at the wrong time that turned us back to the car, but turn we did and home we headed. The long walk in the beautiful forest proved enjoyable, but nothing more, and as we retired for the night our precious bundle was still secure in her comfortable hidey-hole. Sleep came easily as we rested happy in the knowledge that our lives and our baby were in the centre of God's will. After all, not a day had passed but we had placed both into the Lord's hands.

Our next car journey together was only two days later. The scenery on the way was completely different to what we had experienced along the beautiful coast road. This time we travelled through a rather bleak and battered Belfast, during days when armed soldiers still patrolled our streets. The Maternity Hospital was on the then infamous Falls Road, and while many still feared that notorious area, I was used to it, having worked at the Royal site since I was only seventeen. Anyway, I was just glad that at last the obstetrician had decided to intervene, as this baby was oblivious to the fact that she was keeping a lot of people waiting! Philip was entering the unknown. I, on the other hand, as a qualified midwife by now, knew exactly what lay ahead. I wonder who was better off!

After seven and a half hours labour on the 2nd August, 1979 at 1.26am a small dark-haired midwife announced in her broad Scottish accent, "It's a little lassie! You have a bonnie wee daughter!" Our hearts seemed to explode with joy as our little girl was lifted into the air for us to catch our first glimpse of. As I held her close, my heart just flooded with praise to the Saviour who had brought such happiness into our lives. A couple of minutes later she was handed over to Philip, all wrapped up in a warm green towel, her little face wrinkled and her hair still matted. Surely there could not have been a more beautiful sight as she lay quietly in her proud daddy's arms with her tiny (still blue) hands clasped under her chin. Trying out her name for the first time, Philip softly kissed her cheek, "Cheryl," he whispered, "it suits you so well, for you are surely our little 'darling'". If ever a man looked besotted by a baby, it was that man, that day!

By 3am, with Daddy packed off home, Cheryl and I settled down for a short, but peaceful, sleep after our tiring 'labour' experience. As I looked across the room I could hardly believe she was mine – the little kicks I felt for the past months now had a face, and for sure my life would never be the same again. Never before had I felt so complete. Drifting off to sleep I was oblivious to all that lay ahead.

Those days in hospital were a lovely time of 'getting-to-know-you' that preceded a wonderful home-coming. The flat appeared brighter than usual that day, and a large bouquet of summer flowers filled the room with their fresh fragrance. It was granny's way of welcoming home her own daughter and her first grandchild. The fuss that one tiny little baby could bring to a home was enormous, and we were only too pleased to involve all the family. Presents seemed to flood in, and I felt that Cheryl must surely have the biggest wardrobe in Ulster, incorporating every frill and flounce imaginable. The hallway to our flat constantly echoed the sound of happy conversation as night after night friends made their way to welcome the most beautiful addition to our family.

What is it about a newborn baby that creates such emotion? Perhaps it is the sight of perfection in miniature, the tiny toes and fingers displaying even smaller nails; the wrinkled skin that almost looks a little too big to cover such a small frame while feeling softer than the exquisite work of the rarest silk worm. Or maybe it is the unrepeatable expressions that cross her beautiful face as she sleeps, yawns, or stretches in readiness for another feed. Maybe the smell of baby powder mixed with utter dependence on you for their every need causes some kind of a catalyst deep within your being. I don't know. I only know that she brought out something in me that I could never have imagined, and am not eloquent enough to describe. The huge privilege of delivering around forty babies was a tremendous experience, one mixed with anxiety, skill and sheer delight. To participate in such a special moment in the lives of others was indeed precious - yet it paled into insignificance when compared to having this one baby of my own.

My midwifery experience allowed me to avoid many of the concerns of a new mother. Handling Cheryl for whatever reason, be it bathing, washing or feeding, was never fraught with anxiety. It was pure delight. And so I quickly relaxed into the role of motherhood. Or so I thought.

Cheryl being an August baby allowed us to enjoy sunny days and long summer evenings. Perfect opportunity for getting out the rather large and grand pram for leisurely walks, and for showing baby off! On one such day I decided Cheryl and I would walk the mile or so to our local bank to open a savings account for her, as people had been so generous with their gifts. As Cheryl was just fed, I knew we would have plenty of time to get there and back before she woke up, so up the long hilly road we headed on a beautiful sunny afternoon. Cheryl was still sleeping when we reached the bank, and I parked her right outside the door and joined the rather long queue. The time passed fairly quickly as I chatted with some of the people I knew. After handing over the completed form and money, I placed the new savings passbook into my handbag and set off for home.

The return journey was all the quicker because it was down hill and as I put my hand on the door of the entrance hallway sheer panic gripped me. I had left the baby outside the bank! Turning on my heels to run back all kinds of thoughts rushed across my mind. "How could I have been be so stupid! Would she still be there? Maybe someone has kidnapped her! She might be crying and someone will have called the police. Social services will take her away from me. I'm not fit to be a mother! Why did Philip have to be out, he could have taken me up in the car." Sweat, by this time, was mingled with my tears as I sobbed in time with my frantic paces. Only once was I called upon to make up the cross-country team in school, but on this day I think I would have been picked for the Olympics! What a sight I must have looked and sounded as by the time I reached the half-way point I was wheezing like the asthmatic I was. There was no time to stop to look for a hankie or an inhaler. "Please God, please let her be safe!" I cried, all the way to the bank. Before I crossed the road I could see her brown pram in the distance, but it brought me no comfort. "What if the pram was empty? How could I tell Philip that I left his little daughter all on her own surrounded by strangers? As I reached the pram I was afraid to look inside, but in an instant the fear was replaced by relief. Cheryl was still fast asleep, totally unaware of the dreadful mistake her mother had just made.

With a very wet hankie in one hand and holding tightly to my precious cargo with the other I made my way home, yet again... exhausted. It was an important lesson in the folly of over-confidence, and a realization that this little one was going to need more than me to look out for her. "Thank you, God."

She was such a good baby, feeding and sleeping right on cue, and apart from a few hours of walking her through colic each evening, those early months were sheer joy. Smiling came just a little later than the expected six weeks, but, boy, was it worth waiting for! Her blue eyes sparkled in sequence with the rise of the corners of her rosebud lips, while blonde shoots started to appear from her baldy little head. Visits to the grandparents were always a treat, for all of us. Weekly weight and length were discussed, as was whatever beautiful fashion item was worn on that particular day. The first Christmas passed with flash photography in abundance, and even the winter did not seem so miserable that year.

That was until Granny Fraser lowered her voice one day, and with words she obviously did not want to use, said: "Catherine, do you not think Cheryl should be able to hold her head up a bit better by now? She doesn't seem to be reaching for anything." Before I had time to respond, and because I was utterly shocked at the implied suggestion, she continued, "I think she should be showing a wee bit more progress by now, Love, she is nearly five months old." My shock turned to rage as I grabbed the sleeping child out of her doting granny's arms. "How dare you say that Cheryl is slow," I retorted angrily, "I'm the midwife here, you know. All babies progress at different speeds. She's just a typical wee girl. Quiet and gentle. There's absolutely nothing wrong with her!" Granny's tears did nothing to assuage my anger that she should dare think there could possibly be anything wrong with my baby. Granny held her peace, and with Cheryl all tucked up in her pram I quickly made my exit, determined I would never give any more thought to the concerns of one who had seen three of her own safely through childhood.

But the question would not go away, no matter how much I tried. It plagued my every waking moment; kept me up at night; cast a shadow over my soul.

* * *

When I was fourteen years old I had made an amazing discovery. Having watched a school classmate change almost overnight from being a rude, obnoxious kind of character to a genuinely warm and kind girl, I was curious. I had always been the one who never missed church, the one who was quiet and thoughtful, yet this girl talked about knowing Jesus as Saviour in a way I had never heard before. The lurking question of 'what is a real Christian?' was answered one evening when I attended a youth meeting with this girl. Other teenagers used phrases that night that I had not been aware of before. Phrases like 'born again'; 'trusting in Christ'; 'being saved.' I did not understand what it all meant, but I did see something real in their lives that I wanted for myself. They looked happy and satisfied. They seemed to know where they were going in life, and I wanted to head in the same direction. "So being a Christian isn't just a matter of going to church," I quizzed myself as I rushed home, "it's all about knowing Jesus for yourself. How on earth do you do that?"

One amazing fact about God is that He is true to His word, even if we don't know it. As a seeking, rather confused teenager, I didn't know that it said in Jeremiah 29:13, "You will seek Me and find Me, when you search for Me with all your heart." But God did, and when I prayed that night for God to show me how I could get to know Jesus, He gave me a picture of the Cross. For the first time ever I saw that Jesus had died for me, in order that I could get to know Him. All the church-going in the world couldn't make me a Christian. It was 'Christ in' that could make me a brand new person. (2Cor 5:17)

Once my younger sister was asleep, I quietly crept on to my knees at the side of my bed. I didn't know any fancy words, I only knew that my wrong-doing was what had sent Jesus to the Cross, so I asked Him to forgive me and come and live in my life. There was no blinding light, no voice from Heaven, simply a deep sense that God had done what I had asked (John 1:12). It has always puzzled me that so many people think the Christian life to be boring and restrictive. Nothing could be further from the truth. That night started a roller-coaster ride of excitement and deep joy that I wouldn't have swapped with any teenager who was doing all the 'normal' things. I didn't need to do drink or drugs in order to have a good time, and I was always able to remember what I did the next day!

***

Eight years on I could look back and say that I had no regrets. Following Jesus was more than I had ever dreamed. Life was wonderful. The Bible was real and relevant to my everyday living. I had always believed God was in control, and that I could safely leave my life in His hands, but somewhere deep in the recesses of my heart I could feel a little crack forming. It was being chiselled out by a fear that I had hidden away. And the fear had a face - Barbara's face.

Baby clinic was on Thursday. I would ask Janet, my health visitor and friend, if she would have a closer look at Cheryl. Her six month assessment was almost due anyway. Then maybe Granny would believe me. Cheryl was as normal as any other little baby girl.

I had fooled myself into believing that the health checks were merely to dispel these concerns rather than to seek help, and even though we were passed from pillar to post seeing a variety of doctors, I was convinced that each visit was a sensible rather than necessary consultation. Only the reassuring comments were actively remembered. "If it's okay with you Catherine, I'd like a colleague of mine to carry out a formal assessment on Cheryl. As you know I specialize mostly in Neonates now. He's much more up to date with this sort of thing. He'll see you quickly though; there's got to be some perks in the job," suggested the paediatrician. He was someone I knew from midwifery training, and the rest of the conversation was taken up with chat about work. "Surely this would be the last, and I could get on with the job of enjoying my first baby's first year!" I thought, as we headed for home.

True to his word the appointment came quickly although I was shocked with the content of the letter. "Your child has been referred for assessment at the Child Development Clinic." I thought we were going to see a 'colleague', not a whole troupe of people. The letter went on to explain that, "The assessment will last for two and a half hours, with half an hour allocated to each professional." With eyes agog and jaw dropped I read on: Cheryl was to see a paediatrician, a physiotherapist, a speech therapist, an occupational therapist, and a social worker. She was barely seven months old, what on earth did she need to see all these people for?

It was a beautiful spring afternoon as we headed to the hospital. Philip had cleared his diary for the rest of the day and was making reassuring noises as he took on the role of protector for the two ladies in his life. His little daughter may be a bit slow, but she would catch up - just wait and see. Betrayal was playing itself out in my heart, almost as if taking her to this place would change her into something she was not. I held her all the closer with a determination deep inside that I was not going to leave this place without answers. I had had enough of uncertainty.

She looked so beautiful. Teething had put little roses on her cheeks and when she smiled her one little tooth looked like a badge of honour in the middle of a round little face. I was confident that she could not fail to impress in her pink frilly dress, yet as I looked at her tiny fingers tightly locked around mine I prayed: "Please God, let everything be okay." It was a tedious afternoon and I was disappointed that she was scheduled to see the doctor last. After all he was the important one. The frilly dress was removed almost immediately as one by one the different therapists put Cheryl through her paces. She was poked and prodded, and expected to do all kinds of things that, as far as I was concerned, were far too much for a child of seven months old. I answered reams of questions, but, out of character, I asked very few. Cheryl behaved very well and I was so proud of her, but by the time we got to see the doctor she was fretful and tired. "What a pity she couldn't have seen him earlier," I said to my weary husband, "she's just too tired to impress him now."

We were shown into a large room with windows on two sides, draped by long curtains with a bold rose print. There were toys strewn on a mat in the corner, and a large wooden tricycle that looked as if it had been made by hand. The room was dishevelled, witness to the fact that we were the last to be seen at the clinic. The paediatrician was a tall, slim, grandfatherly figure of a man, and when he smiled his eyes sparkled and the surrounding laughter lines gave away his friendly nature, and put us at our ease. "So this is Cheryl," he said gently as he lifted her out of my arms, "you have had a busy day, Little One, it's no wonder you are feeling a bit sad." I watched with amazement as he totally ignored us and took our tear-stained little girl on a walk around the room. He tenderly kissed her forehead and cheek to cheek he talked to her in hushed tones. The calming melody of his voice stopped her crying, and the secure hold he had on her gave both her and us the assurance that she was safe in his arms. "Here was a man who clearly had a lifetime of experience with children," I thought, "he loves them, and they love him." He held her for nearly the whole time we were with him, every now and then rocking her when she showed any sign of unrest. Apart from that he did nothing else with her. There were questions for us of course as he flicked through the rest of the reports from the previous assessors.

"You can dress her now," he said as he put her back into my arms. "The physio has asked for hip x-rays, and you can have that done before you go home today. She will be in contact soon to arrange an appointment at the physio department. See you in six months time." X-rays, physio, appointments! It was time to take the bull by the horns. "Is there a problem? She will pick up, won't she?" I asked, and as I did so the doctor leaned forward in amazement as if I had just uttered the most ridiculous question he had ever heard.

I braced myself for the answer as this kindly gentleman seemed to undergo a kind of metamorphosis as he towered over us, changing into a clarion of doom. The words he uttered crashed in on us like a verbal baseball bat wreaking havoc on our lives: "Mrs. Campbell, don't you realize, your little girl is severely handicapped?" he said incredulously, "she will never be normal." I gasped in disbelief and shock, my head was spinning, my heart was thumping and I was trying, with little success, to hold back a dam of tears. He was still talking, but his voice was far away as if he was in another room, something about us having seen three doctors and did none of them tell us that Cheryl had microcephaly? Her brain hadn't grown properly and that's why she has such a small head. My life was falling apart in front of me, "Never be normal" was all I could hear, and I was sure if we could only get away from this man everything would go back to the way it was before we entered this awful place. "Never be normal", thundered in my head in time to the thumping of my heart. The panic and need to escape reached a crescendo. He was still talking as I made for the door, apologizing this time that we had to receive such bad news in this way.

The silence in the car was only broken by my stifled sobs. My brain was in overdrive trying to process all the information we had received in the past few months. How could they not have told me? Why didn't I ask more questions along the way? Everyone who had seen her was always measuring her head, why was I only picking up on that now? Ever since Barbara I had been on the lookout for the big head, the sign of hydrocephalus, and when I first set eyes on my darling daughter I was so pleased that hers was small and dainty. How could I have missed it? "Never be normal", he said, "how can we tell our parents that their first, beautiful grandchild would 'never be normal'?" I didn't realize that my last thoughts were spoken aloud until Philip's reply interrupted them. "He could be wrong Catherine. She's only a bit slow and we'll work hard with her, she will catch up, just you wait and see. God will make it alright." Then I caught a glimpse of his face in the rear-view mirror. My poor Philip, my dear, dear, husband. His eyes portrayed a look of deep pain, a helplessness, totally unaware of how, as the head of this family, he could fix the disaster that had arrived on his lap. Daddies were meant to be able to fix anything, husbands were meant to be the protectors of their wives, at least that was what all the good parenting books had said. Now in this moment, denial was the best thing he could come up with, and I loved him even for that.

How could it all go so horribly wrong? How could we leave our beautiful happy home one lunch-time and return at tea-time with our lives completely turned upside down? How could we go out with a few concerns about our firstborn and return with a different child? A child with whom there would be none of the usual guarantees, except one. "She would never be normal." We moved from the sunshine of a trouble-free life to the darkness of the fiercest storm as if we had been dropped over a cliff, and there was no rescue in sight.

The family were heartbroken, but they jumped right in to support and love us even more than before. Cheryl was totally oblivious to all that was going on around her and hot tears splashing on to her cheeks at regular intervals only brought a smile. She wasn't a different child, rather exactly the same beautiful, blue-eyed blonde that we had come to know and love for the previous seven months. Even my anger at not knowing sooner was cooled by the fact that we had been given all that time to get to know her before the bomb-shell was dropped. For that I will forever be grateful.

Bad news travels fast. In no time at all our friendly neighbourhood and church family were in a state of shock. It was almost as if a death had taken place, and everyone was in mourning. Thoughtful whispers and caring glances followed us wherever we went. Our sad news may have been the talk of the neighbourhood but I knew it wasn't merely gossip, rather that "Such a lovely young couple should be burdened with such sad news", as I overheard on more than one occasion. The hallway to our flat was once again busy night after night as people made their little pilgrimages to see us. This time joyful laughter was replaced by hushed tones. For some a hug and tears were enough to assure us of their love, while others felt a need to leave a verse of scripture with us to convince us of God's love. Very soon however, this began to grate on me, as my broken heart could no more understand what God was doing, than any of these friends could understand what I was going through. As soon as a Bible was opened I felt as if I had been stood in front of a firing squad, verses hitting me with the speed of a machine gun. If one more person said: "All things work together for good to those who love God, to those who are called according to His purpose" (Rom 8:28), I think I would have hit them! It was a real lesson to me in how and when to quote scripture at people!

But somehow when **God** whispers His Word to your heart that's a completely different matter.

From early on we are conditioned to the wearing of masks, especially in the Christian church. Fear of not living up to others' expectations, alongside a genuine wish not to let the Lord down, tricks us into showing people what we think they want to see. For me that meant I should put on my smile with my Sunday-go-to-meeting clothes, and respond with the words "I'm fine" when people ask: "how are you?" After all, my husband was a preacher and it wouldn't do for people to see his wife fall apart, or to hear the anguish of her heart as she pleaded with God every day for a miracle. Few knew of the nights I cried myself to sleep, and I often even kept those tears for the nights Philip was away on evangelistic business. As far as I was concerned, Cheryl's diagnosis could not possibly be in God's will for our lives. I had never felt so out of control or so unsure of God's love or purposes. And so I would cover my head with the duvet, and cry out to God every night. "God," I would say, "I don't know what you're doing with my life. Please help me."

On one such evening, Philip was away, and Cheryl was fast asleep. I was in my usual position, weeping and praying, when God crept into my room, and whispered His word to my aching heart. The words that He used had been hidden deep in my heart from shortly after I was saved. They were words that blew me away, because, as a young Christian I thought, "With a God like this you could change the world." And in the darkness of that room and of my soul, He reminded me of the promise I had read years before. "Catherine," He said as clearly as if He had been sitting beside me, "Fear not, you are mine. When you pass through the waters, I will be with you; and through the rivers, they shall not overflow you. When you walk through the fire you shall not be burned, for I am the Lord your God."(Isaiah 43:1-3) I pulled the covers off my head almost expecting to see Him because His voice was so clear, and for the first time in weeks I felt His presence binding up the pain in my heart. Peace flooded the room. He did love me after all. What was it He said? "Don't be afraid, you belong to Me. In all these 'waters' of suffering I am going to be right there with you. You will never be alone." Oh, the peace that brought to my heart! My first rainbow, right in the middle of the storm, was the promise of His presence. Just as God had put a rainbow right in the thing that Noah feared most, the cloud, so God had placed His promise in the thing I feared most, the unknown. God had not deserted me after all. The only niggle in my mind as I settled for sleep was the mention of "rivers" and "fire". Surely that didn't mean there was more ahead?

Babies and early mornings are synonymous. But I didn't mind, as I couldn't wait to check out those verses in Isaiah. The sense of peace had remained through the night and with tea in hand and Bible on knee, I searched the scriptures for myself. "How could I have got it so wrong?" I said, beating the air with my words as I read, "nowhere does God promise us a trouble-free life." I moved from Isaiah to Job and read: "Man is born to trouble as the sparks fly upwards,"(Job 5:7) and on to Matthew 5:45 where Jesus says: "He sends rain on the just and the unjust." As I thought about these words I remembered a bookmark a friend had given me some time before. It talked about 'God not promising us skies ever blue' and something about no 'joy without sorrow or peace without pain'. Why did I think that just because we loved God that nothing bad could ever happen to us? An avid reader, I had read many books of missionaries who had suffered greatly. If bad things happened to these giants of the faith, what made me think there was some exemption clause written into my life. How easily we fall into the devil's trap of the prosperity gospel —"follow Christ and everything will turn out your way." Then when the promise fails, we experience disappointment with God. And those of us who are disappointed with God are easily turned away from the narrow path.

As I finished my tea, I knew that God's promise was true: He would be with me; I would never have to walk this journey alone. But I also knew something I had chosen to ignore until now; pain is part of the human package, even for the Christian. Cheryl was still handicapped. As I closed my Bible I vowed I would keep on praying, and maybe God would change His mind.

When Cheryl was around six months old I had returned to work with the offer of two nights a week in Coronary Care, rather than full-time hours in Midwifery. This way I could have the best of both worlds; precious time with my daughter, and a job that I found exciting and that also helped with the family finances. Normally I got a lift home in the morning, but on this particular day I had to take the bus. Tiredness has a way of lowering your guard, and as I sat on the bus I was exhausted and feeling a bit sorry for myself. Added to which, the bus was crawling at a snails pace along the route, picking up passengers at every stop.

Agitation was setting in when the bus stopped yet again, but I noticed the people in front of me adjusting their positions. A few of them moved to the aisle seat, while others shuffled uncomfortably, setting their bags or newspapers on the seats next to them. I was puzzled. The young man who had just boarded was chatting loudly to the driver as he purchased his ticket. He carried a large plastic lunchbox under his arm, and smiled broadly as he made his way down the aisle, shouting "Hello" to anyone who would take their eyes off the windows and make contact with his face. His slightly slanted eyes, low set ears and thickness of speech gave away the fact that he had Down's syndrome. Suddenly it all made sense. Shuffling around, bags on seats, made it clear that no-one wanted him to sit beside them. He was different, and the rejection of the different made me feel ashamed. As he reached my seat I smiled at him and said "Hello". His face almost parted with the huge grin he made in response, and he walked straight to the back seat, where, my guess is, he sat every morning. And as handbags and newspapers were put back in place, the tears came. "Maybe one day people will treat my little girl with the same disdain," I thought as I tried to compose myself. The picture of such blatant rejection forming in my mind was difficult to bear. This random group of people on the bus had made one thing clear – 'different' is not acceptable.

Two

Designer Made?

THE old adage "love is blind" has been used as an excuse down through the centuries by people who refuse, or are slow, to see the faults in someone else simply because of their love for them.   We have all witnessed a marriage break-up, and were bewildered that 'she didn't see it coming'. But then she loved him…and "love is blind". We have listened on the news to some poor mother testify that "her son was a good boy", when the evidence reveals him to be a murderer. But then she loved him…and "love is blind". For seven months I was convinced that I had the most beautiful, normal daughter in the world. Other people, even my own mother, thought differently. But then I loved her…and "love is blind".

How could I not have seen it? Just like the boy on the bus, Cheryl was different.   A number of our friends had babies that year, and I foolishly thought how lovely it was that Cheryl was still such a cuddly baby, while the others struggled at times when being held. Each child would strive for independence at the simplest of things, from holding its own feeding cup to reaching for the favourite toy. Cheryl, on the other hand, had always been the quiet gentle little girl who relished all the attention others gave her, and never screamed in temper at something she couldn't reach. In fact, she never reached for anything. And I didn't notice. All her little baby friends had strong, big heads, while she had a dainty little one covered with lovely blonde hair. "No problem," I thought, "they are boys after all." And I was glad that her head was small, as she seemed to find it so hard to hold up without help. When I went to lift one of my friends' children, they almost rose up to meet me. Cheryl, on the other hand, would have slipped through my hands like a rag doll if I hadn't held on to her tightly. Yet I refused to let it register in my heart. Her hands were always tightly closed, yet she was unable to hold on to a toy by herself. 'She'll get the hang of it sometime,' I told myself. One thing she could do really well, though, was smile, and what a smile! The whole room lit up when Cheryl smiled, and when you tickled her knees she threw back her head and laughed! Just like every other baby! And for some reason, this normally astute nurse was completely blind to the fact that her baby was different. In fact her baby had major developmental problems. But then I loved her…and "love is blind".

Cheryl's diagnosis of microcephaly brought things back into sharp focus for me. The condition meant her brain had stopped growing during my pregnancy, and her developmental progress would depend on how much functioning brain was operating normally. Conversely the degree of disability would depend on which areas of the brain were missing or damaged. At this stage no-one could tell us what kind of outcome to expect with Cheryl. However, the paediatrician's statement of "She will never be normal" echoed in my mind like the throbbing of a bad headache.

Having delivered over forty babies, and given birth myself, it goes without saying that after a baby is born the mother's first question, after finding out if it is a boy or girl, is: "Is he (or she) alright?" In the majority of cases the reply is also usually standard: "He (or she) is just perfect."

Those words cause a communal sigh in the delivery room. After all that is what everyone wants…a perfect baby. In fact we live in a world obsessed with perfection, or at least its notion of perfection. Many of us strive relentlessly to achieve academic success, that will in turn open up the perfect job opportunities, that will give us the financial capabilities to buy the big house filled with the perfect size zero wife and equally good looking children. They, in their turn, will strive relentlessly to achieve academic success, and on it goes. The rest of us look on and wish we could have a share in their seemingly perfect life, and spend our time trying to dip our toes into what we regard as perfection.

We, undoubtedly, live in the world of the designer label. What we wear is not nearly as important as who made it, and that others know who made it! So much so, that manufacturers now display the label on the *outside* of the garment. Why wear Ralph Lauren or Coco Chanel if no-one else recognises it? Many of our teenagers would rather die than be seen in a pair of trainers manufactured by anyone other than those of the current trendsetting brands. The goal of perfection invades many areas of our lives, not least what we wish for our children. We long for them to be perfect; to be healthy; to be successful, and to be liked by others. I was no different. And when things don't turn out the way you expect it has to be someone's fault.

I wish I could say that I accepted Cheryl's condition without question, as so many other godly people accept dark and difficult circumstances, but I didn't. It is obvious to me now that I was just beginning to walk the long road of learning unquestioning faith. Then, at just twenty three years old, I was tormented by questions that had no answers. The blame game is a dangerous one to play, and one that has no winners. What surprised me was the number of other players in my particular game. Players who had little previous involvement in my life, yet their cunning and often unwitting tactics added to the suffering of my soul. It amazed me the throwaway, hurtful and negative comments that seemed to cast a cloud over the encouraging murmurings of those who cared deeply about my pain.

"Why did God give your Catherine a child like that?" my mother was asked. "When you think of all the evil women in the world today, and your Catherine's such a good girl." Mum warded off the comment with the disdain it deserved, but as I held Cheryl after hearing those words I was astounded that someone would think of Cheryl as unworthy or not good enough for our family.

A child's first birthday usually brings the next big influx of cards after the birth itself, but as news filtered through to friends across the world, we received little notes of encouragement and assurances of prayer long before that date. Having many missionary friends and others in Christian ministry at home has always been a source of delight. The ability to share with likeminded people has often helped to reduce the burdens you are unable to share with those you are ministering to. On one day a letter arrived with a foreign postmark that gave away the sender, and as I tore open the envelope I wondered who had told them our news. The world is definitely a small place!

"Must be a sermon," I thought, "as there seems to be masses of paper here." A small cotton handkerchief trimmed with orange embroidery floated to the floor as I unfolded the paper. "Strange," I thought, as I settled myself down to read the epistle. It started with the usual greetings and I was touched by the sentiments, but it wasn't long before my jaw dropped and hot tears were stinging my face. The author was setting himself up as a messenger from God to tell us that it was not God's will for Cheryl to be this way, and therefore there must be some sin in our lives that was bringing judgement on our family. We were to get on our knees and pray that God would reveal our sin, and after we repented, God would heal Cheryl. In the meantime, if we placed the handkerchief, that he had prayed over, on top of Cheryl, God would answer his prayer and start the healing process. At one time this person had had an important spiritual influence on our lives, and although contact had been only sporadic in the time leading up to the letter, I was shocked and further pained by his words. By the time my husband arrived home my hurt had turned to anger, and yet I was afraid that there might be some truth in what he said. What if Cheryl was handicapped because of something we had done? What if it was our fault? And if we didn't put the handkerchief on Cheryl could we be disobeying God?

Philip and I are so different. He is quiet and gentle, always prepared to look at what lies behind someone's actions, and not to jump quickly in judgement. At times it infuriates me, and at times I envy his measured and cautious approach. It usually means less repentance time for him, and much more for me!

He read the letter in silence, only the odd sigh hissing from his pursed lips. He was disappointed in what was written, even hurt; and after taking a torrent of anger from me, he took me in his arms and let me cry. (He's been very good at that over the years.) Then when the dust had settled, we discussed the comments made in our unwelcome correspondence.

There is no doubt that scripture makes clear that none of us are as we should be, because of original sin (Gen 3), and it can be proven medically that some sickness develops because of certain kinds of immoral living. But Jesus clearly tells his disciples in John 9 that personal sickness is not necessarily a direct result of another's sin. The disciples asked Jesus if the man was born blind because of his parent's sin, and Jesus answered, "Neither this man nor his parents sinned, but this happened so that the works of God may be displayed in his life."(NIV) If any lesson can be drawn from this story, it is surely that sickness is more to do with the eternal plan of God than the current circumstances of an individual's life. This went some way to lowering the accusing finger that had tried to point blame in our direction.

"What should we do with this?" I asked my husband as I stared at the crumpled handkerchief sitting in my lap. Only once in scripture was there mention of people being healed after a handkerchief had been sent to them; yet I did not feel that the sender in this case warranted the same authority as that given in Acts 19:11&12. "Now God worked unusual miracles by the hands of Paul, so that even handkerchiefs or aprons were brought from his body to the sick, and the diseases left them..." These were 'unusual miracles', and while I do believe that God can still heal today, the accompanying misinterpretation of scripture in our letter did nothing to give me any confidence in this limp piece of cotton.

Comments come and comments go, and I was much too busy to let them linger in the open, so they were often filed in the subconscious to fritter away or to be dealt with at a later date. How vulnerable is the hurting heart! Philip has a speech principle that is so wholesome: "If it doesn't edify or exhort, then make sure you need to say it before you do." If only we could all be so wise.

* * *

It is said that a first baby requires you to make lots of adjustments to your life. That's very true. Along with the normal newness of parenting came a whole different set of people and situations that we hadn't reckoned on. Because of my job, hospitals held no major fears for me, but I was amazed at the number of appointments, clinics and professionals that were suddenly involved in our lives. On one day alone five different health professionals arrived at our home within the space of half an hour! The Campbells really had entered the disability lane of a world that, until now, we only knew existed, but never imagined we would be part of. In this world we were to meet remarkable children, loving parents, dedicated staff and those whose job was to solve the strangest of problems with their technical skills. At times we grumbled when we thought the service was inadequate, but in truth, we don't know what we would have done without the therapists who taught us how to work with Cheryl.

The therapy clinics quickly became part of our lives, and we are still in contact with some of the staff we met back then. When you work 'hands-on' with a child over a long period of time it's hard not to make a personal connection. What was passed on at the clinics became the basis for Cheryl's daily routine of physiotherapy, handling and even feeding. Who would have thought that how you eat can affect your ability to make sounds, and even formulate speech; or that how you are positioned for feeding can prevent you from getting pneumonia! For me, it was certainly a case of learning something new every day!

Medical outpatient clinics were a different kettle of fish. Generally speaking, very good relationships were formed over a number of years with the paediatricians who cared for Cheryl, but the forays to see consultants at predominately adult hospitals were very stressful for both mother and child.

Cheryl's beautiful blue eyes looked normal, yet her visual response was slow. Only when a toy or shiny object was held close to her face did it stimulate any kind of a reaction. Sometimes we wondered if she did not reach for things because she found it difficult to do so, or because she could not see what we were waving in front of her. Wanting to give her every opportunity for progress, I was happy when the day for the appointment at the Eye Department of a major hospital arrived.

Philip dropped us at the front entrance, and drove off to speak at an afternoon ladies meeting, apologizing as he went for not being able to accompany us. "No problem," I assured him, "I'm not expecting anything mind-blowing today. See you later." Cheryl was snug and asleep when we reached what I can only describe as a chaotic and crowded waiting area. After some time had passed a hassled nurse called Cheryl's name. Explaining that her pupils would need to be dilated before the doctor saw her, she showed us into a rather square room with seats on three sides. The lighting was dimmed to reduce the discomfort of those who were waiting for their eye drops to work. It was also crowded, and I squashed into a seat between two people. Before I had time to lift Cheryl out of the buggy, the nurse had hurriedly put the drops into her eyes. Shocked, and with stinging eyes she woke with a start, her crying the only noise to break the silence of this uncomfortable room. I began to wonder if no-one had ever heard a crying baby before, as people bristled and stiffened while I tried to calm my frightened daughter.

At the end of the room were two curtained cubicles. Some patients disappeared behind the curtains, while others were whisked away somewhere else. Those of us who remained, we could hear every word that passed between doctor and patient, including diagnosis and personal details. "So much for confidentiality," I thought.

The curtain was pulled back, and Cheryl's name was called once more. With baby in one arm, and pushing the buggy with the other, I moved forward with difficulty, as the room continued to fill with an endless stream of patients. After a brief hello, the doctor quickly read the referral letter, and disappeared through an adjoining door. Some time passed, and he returned with a man who I can only assume was the consultant, as we were never introduced. The tell-tale accompanying entourage of medical students confirmed my suspicions; "How on earth are they all going to fit into this cubicle?" was my silent question. They weren't! The curtain remained undrawn, leaving my private concerns and vulnerability visible to every person in the room. With nowhere else to look, and no escape, they were all drawn into a conversation they did not want to hear, no doubt longing for the proverbial big hole to swallow them up from the view of this distraught young mother.

"So you are concerned about her sight," the doctor said and, without waiting for a reply, he turned to the waiting students, "What do you notice about this child?" "Come-on," he grunted, "it's very obvious." Someone cleared their throat at the back of the group, "She has a small head," he said. "Hold her up straight, Mum. What else do you notice about her small head?" he cajoled them. By now I felt invisible, and my daughter a mere teaching aid in the hands of a learned but insensitive man. "It's flat at the back," was another's reply. "Exactly," said the eye specialist, and without as much as a hesitation, or concern at what he was going to say in a public place about my child, he launched into the next part of his lecture. He was talking to them, I was merely listening in, as he explained how the vision centre had not developed in the brain, and could therefore not translate what was being sent to it from the eyes. For the first time he looked at me, and said, "Your daughter has cortical blindness; nothing wrong with her eyes, it's just that she can't make sense of what is coming through them. No need to make another appointment, there is nothing we can do for her." And with the flick of his hand a path was made for his retreat.

A more subdued and somewhat embarrassed nurse helped me back to a seat, while the other shocked onlookers held their collective breath. As I struggled to put Cheryl's coat on, and hold myself together, the elderly lady beside me made a try at the only humanity I experienced that afternoon. With her hand on my knee she said, "I'm so sorry Love, for your bad news." I don't know how I managed to get out of that department with dry eyes. Outside the rain mingled with my tears, and the passers-by didn't seem to notice as they rushed to seek shelter.

Philip had seen us coming in the rear view mirror, and jumped out of the car to rescue us from the downpour. His smile quickly disappeared on realizing that it was more than rain that soaked his wife. I sat behind him in the car, holding Cheryl's hand as she sat in the car seat. "She can't see," I blubbered, "or rather, her brain can't make sense of what her eyes let in." "But her eyes are okay?" Philip questioned. "Yes, but the doctor says that doesn't matter because her brain doesn't know what she's seeing." As I heard myself use the words 'cortical blindness' it was all too much to take in, "doesn't she have enough to cope with, without being blind as well?" Philip did not reply. But Heaven did…

It was as if God heard the anguish of my soul, and responded in a way I have only experienced a few times in my life. There was an almost physical presence in the car; and I felt the peace of God wash over me from head to foot, calming me intimately, and causing the weight in my chest to disappear. It felt like a bucket of cool water pouring over me on a hot day, relieving every sense. All that was left was an overwhelming sense of the love of God, and a tangible experience of Philippians 4:7; "And the peace of God, which surpasses all understanding, will guard your hearts and minds through Christ Jesus." By the time we reached home God's peace far outweighed any pain inflicted by an uncaring doctor, or unwanted diagnosis. Anyway, no-one knew for sure precisely how much Cheryl could or could not see, so we went on treating her like a sighted child, stimulating her whenever, and however, possible.

* * *

The Campbells love birthdays, and as we were due to be away over Cheryl's first birthday, there simply had to be an extra celebration. Grannies, granddads, aunts and uncles, and a few visiting foreign friends all gathered for the big party in our rather small living room. Cheryl was in her element. She looked stunning in her elegant party dress, with accompanying lacy socks and enough shiny blonde hair to now cover her whole head. Like any other little girl, she played the crowd that day, charming everyone in sight. You would have thought she knew she was the main attraction, smiling right on cue, and throwing her head back with a chuckle every time her knees were tickled. It was a genuinely wonderful day, and the many sad moments of the past year seemed to blow away with the flame on the candle of her large birthday cake. As I tucked her up in her cot, after the visitors had gone, I felt the delight a firstborn gives. Others may have looked on her as different, but to me she was simply 'my Cheryl'.

"It will be nice to get away," I said to myself, as I packed what seemed to be an inordinate amount of stuff for such a little person. I managed to convince myself that it would all be needed, so nothing was retrieved from the overfilled suitcase. We were off to help staff the TES family holiday centre, where over two hundred people would come on each of the three weeks for fun and bible ministry. Most of the evangelists and their wives were roped into helping, and you could end up cleaning, helping in the kitchen, or on the games field! Based at a private boarding school in the English countryside, it was certainly not a holiday for the staff, but they do say that 'a change is as good as a rest', and that's just what I needed. I could make myself useful in the kitchen when I wasn't busy with Cheryl. The journey was tedious, but as we turned into the long, tree-lined driveway I thought I'd never seen anything as beautiful in my life. The building that lay before us was majestic, and I could just imagine the rich and famous leaving their sons to study in such elegance. That is, until we saw the dorms, and then I thought we had been transferred to one of Her Majesty's prisons. They were unbelievably tawdry! At least we only had to sleep in them!

Work was quickly underway, as guests started to arrive. Families came from all over England, with a number of small church groups. One such group was from a Nigerian church based in London, and they had brought a number of babies and toddlers with them. There was a lovely enclosed garden, which was used as a creche while the morning bible studies were in progress. The weather was beautiful, and so I decided to take Cheryl, in her buggy, to meet the other little ones. On the path leading into the garden, I was approached by a rather large lady in quite impressive Nigerian dress. I smiled as we met, only to hear her tutting in response. Before I could speak a greeting she spoke, vigorously shaking her head as she did so. "Shame, shame," she said, "children like that shouldn't be born. Taint right. Better if she'd died at birth, don't you think?" Dumbfounded, I stammered, "No I *don't* think so." My retreat was instant, and I virtually ran through the maze of corridors to our awful little room.

"How could anyone look at you and think it would be better if you had never been born," I said to Cheryl, glad that she could never be hurt by another's words, because she was oblivious to their meaning. In that instant I refused to believe she was some freak of nature, or even some kind of divine mistake. "Surely they're wrong, Lord?" I questioned, as the old dorm bed creaked under my weight. "Show me they're wrong, Lord," I pleaded, as I lifted my bible on to my knee. It was one of those moments when I wish I'd known my bible better; known where to turn to get just the answer I needed. But the Author of the book knew better than the reader what was needed at that moment.

I do not normally agree with the ad hoc approach of throwing your bible open and hoping a verse jumps up and hits you between the eyes. Taking that as divine guidance is shaky, to say the least. Far better to be regularly in the Word, and to hear God speaking, than to use it as some kind of a quick fix to give you the answers you want to hear. Yet God, who recognizes, not only our immediate needs, but our weakness in times of despair, occasionally displays His graciousness by speaking to us out of the unusual. Such was the case that day.

My bible opened naturally in the Psalms; not surprising really as David's poetry is easy to read when concentration is poor, as mine had been in the previous months. I sighed, not really expecting to find what I was looking for there, and wondering if I should maybe turn to the book of Job, but I read on anyway.....and this is what I read in Psalm 139:13-16:

"For you formed my inward parts; You covered me in my mother's womb.
I will praise You, for I am fearfully and wonderfully made;
Marvellous are Your works, and that my soul knows very well.
My frame was not hidden from You, when I was made in secret,
And skilfully wrought in the lowest parts of the earth.
Your eyes saw my substance, being yet unformed.
And in Your book they were all written, the days fashioned for me,
When as yet there were none of them."

"Listen to this Cheryl," I exclaimed, making the poor child jump as I raised my voice in excitement. "You are no mistake, sweetheart, God knew exactly what He was doing when He made you….it says so right here in Psalm 139. It says here that God formed you; He knew your little frame before I did, when it was just a bunch of cells – it wasn't hidden from Him. You were no surprise to Him. And, you know what, Cheryl? God knows exactly how many days we will have you. You were meant to live, and not to die. That lady was wrong, very wrong!" I doubt she understood a word I was saying, but the excitement in her mummy's voice made a big smile cross her face. We danced around the room together; sure that God had not made some big faux pas with my daughter. I may not have understood why He made her the way He did, but the knowledge of the sovereign hand of God from her conception put paid to the nonsense that she was some unfortunate disaster.

Down through the years I have learned to see this world's view of perfection from a completely different perspective. Our 'raison d'etre' is far greater than health and wealth, happiness and beauty. Psalm 139 gave me the assurance that Cheryl was "*Designer*" made, and that stamped across her life were the words: '**MADE WITH LOVE BY GOD**.'

Three
Changing Direction

THE TES Holiday Centre was full of highs and lows for three long weeks. I had experienced the euphoria that accompanied the knowledge that Cheryl was no mistake. Somehow God had a reason for her being as she was, yet alongside this was a reluctance to fully accept that she might never walk or talk. It is funny how the human psyche holds tenaciously on to the slimmest strands of hope. A doctor can take the time to explain all the possible scenarios of a particular condition, yet often the patient only remembers the one good thing he has said. It is an emotional protection mechanism. One I have often used myself.

At the time of diagnosis, one of the paediatricians made a comment that I had turned on its heels. "If Cheryl doesn't sit up by the time she is one," he said, "then there will be a serious question mark over her physical development." I had decided to miss the negative implications, and go straight for the positive. "Then there is a chance that she might only be affected mentally," I had thought, "she might even walk, if only she can sit up by her birthday." So we worked with her day in, day out. Poor Cheryl was tormented by physiotherapy, and she hated it! But secretly, my plan was to get her to sit up by that magical first birthday, and then everything would be okay.

She reached one year old during our time at the Holiday Centre. The early family birthday was boosted by a surprise party given by the staff, who had come to love her. Cake, balloons, and a big teddy; accompanied by cuddles and singing, brought lots of smiles from Cheryl, which further excited her admirers! All the attention that was lavished on her helped take the focus away from me; and I was glad. It was hard to keep up the happy act that was hiding a very hurting heart.

Cheryl had reached that important milestone, spoken of by the consultant months before. She was now one...and she couldn't sit up by herself...in fact, she couldn't even hold her own head up without help. That could only mean one thing – there was now a question mark over her physical development. The next day I volunteered to chop the onions...onions for chutney for 250 people...lots of onions, and no need to explain the tears!

Onion chopping was done in a tiny little prep room, cum store, off the main kitchen, hidden from the view of the other workers. The only visitor was the kitchen porter; a humble, godly man, who, although highly intelligent, worked his holidays as a general dogsbody to serve the staff, guests and ultimately the Lord. "Can I help?" he asked. I replied that I was managing okay, wishing he would just go away. "I'm not talking onions," he commented, "can I help with whatever is upsetting you?" He quietly leaned against the bench, with his arms folded, awaiting my reply. I surprised myself by telling far more than expected to someone I had only met two weeks ago. Out it all came; the stuff about the birthday; my disappointment, even anger with God; my longing for Cheryl to be normal, and my deep annoyance with myself for crying so much. "I'm a Christian," I blurted out, "I shouldn't be falling apart like this!"

He was silent for a moment, while I blew my nose yet again, suddenly embarrassed at just how much I had revealed. Most men have difficulty knowing what to do with their own wives when they are emotional, never mind someone else's wife! His response was both gentle, and strong. "Do you believe that God made you?" "Yes," I replied, rather bemused. "Do you believe God made you with tears?" "Of course," I retorted. "Then, if God made you with tears, it is perfectly okay to use them!" he said, shrugging his shoulders. "No guilt required. The rest God will deal with in time, as long as you let Him." His response was short, sweet and simple. No wagging finger of blame, no theological treatise on the sovereignty of God; just simple, loving advice from a compassionate heart. Afterwards he put his bony hand on my shoulder and prayed an equally simple prayer. "Lord, heal Catherine's broken heart. Amen."

Here was a man who understood how disappointment and difficulty affects the human heart, and he didn't make a drama out of a crisis! Peace returned, the onions were chopped, and the conversation between us was never mentioned again.

Dealing over the years with the constant ebb and flow of human emotions, has been personally frustrating, and perhaps even difficult for the onlooker to understand. One minute I experience the highs of God's peace and presence in my life, while at others I am wallowing in the depths of despair. There seems to be such inconsistency. However, I have come to realise that with the constantly changing circumstances surrounding Cheryl's condition, my reactions have merely been that of a mother! We have been created human, with all that involves – joy and sorrow; peace and pain. What I find astounding is the patience of the Creator, as He consistently picks me up, dusts me down, and helps me on my way again. With the passage of time I notice less despairing and more trusting, as I very slowly learn the lessons He is trying to teach me. It is so good to be able to look at the great heroes of scripture, like King David, and identify with their somewhat yo-yo existence. The fact that God did not give up on them fills me with hope!

Apart from the emotional and physical load Cheryl's condition placed on us, we were soon to realise that it wasn't only our dreams for Cheryl that were broken. Since our late teens, both Philip and I felt a real tug towards missionary work abroad. Philip studied Missiology at Bible College, while I completed my Nursing training; all with the intention of being prepared to work in some country of God's choosing overseas. That dream was never to be realized. What Missionary Society would employ a couple with a disabled child? What parent would take their disabled child away from where she could get the best possible treatment?

We would have to learn to dream new dreams, and to accept a change in direction for our lives.

* * *

One month after the fateful first birthday, Cheryl had her first operation. The jerking, writhing movements of her muscles (athetosis), meant that her hip was not able to sit properly in its socket. If Cheryl was ever to stand, even with support, the surgery was necessary, and so we agreed to let it take place. For three months Cheryl was in a huge plaster cast, from her ankles to under her arms, with both legs spread out and bent up like a frog! What a head-turner she was, as we had to fill her pram with pillows and strap her on top, with both legs hanging out over the side! If it hadn't been so serious it would have been comical! What were comical however, were the surprised looks we got as we ventured out for walks together! There were nearly a few others joining Cheryl in plaster as they engaged in rubbernecking to witness this unusual spectacle!

Those three months in plaster were followed by six months in similarly shaped splints, which for a child who could nothing for herself, proved extremely difficult. Sleepless nights rolled into sleepless days, ad infinitum.

However, it was during these days that I became pregnant with our second child. Sometime previously we had visited the geneticist to find out our chances of having a normal brother or sister for Cheryl. He was a lovely man, who gave you his undivided attention while you were with him. He even wrote upside down, to enable you to read his notes, as he was explaining the difficult subject of how genetic anomalies cause abnormal births. There was no way to prove that Cheryl's microcephaly was definitely a genetic problem, as there was not a specific test available. It was his opinion, however, that it was a recessive gene disorder with a 1:5 chance at worse, or a 1:10 chance at best, of recurrence. A 1:10 risk did not sound too bad to me, and a healthy baby would make it all worthwhile.

After talking it over and praying, Philip and I decided that whatever the outcome, we would have the baby. There was no discussion, at any time, of a termination, whatever the test results would show. God's word had already done its work in our hearts concerning the sanctity of human life, and interestingly enough I was not overly concerned during my pregnancy. I was happy, puffy (!), excited and very tired throughout my second pregnancy. Cheryl didn't seem to notice my expanding waistline, or at least she was still able to have her cuddles, and that's all that mattered to her! Also, granny and granda took the extra strain as I grew larger, and they enjoyed every minute of it!

Extra visits to a special genetic obstetric clinic were slotted into my antenatal care, and they helped to encourage us that everything was going along just fine. The baby's head seemed to be growing at the expected rate, which was the only way microcephaly could be detected at this stage. Other tests for various deviations from normal all came up negative, causing a little whoop of glee after each hospital appointment! I enjoyed being pregnant, and a December baby was going to add to the excitement I always have in the run up to Christmas. Cheryl's splints came off in July, making life much easier for everyone, especially her. Life was particularly lovely that autumn, and it was so nice for the whole family to share in the 'normal', after supporting us through the heartache of the previous two years. We wanted them to have a healthy baby to enjoy as well; although their love, acceptance and devotion to Cheryl were always clear for the world to see. Only the visit of the TES Director of Evangelism, Philip's boss, in November stood between us and the big event, and we were even looking forward to that!

Bob's visit came around quicker than expected. He was to stay with us for the first few days of the week, and then go on to the other TES Evangelist for the rest of his time in the Province. Preparing for his visit was quite convenient; as it meant the house would have its final 'big' clean before my due date, which was ten days away. Philip had just left for the airport when I noticed the discomfort in my back... "Too much cleaning," I thought. Promising myself a relaxing evening while they attended their first meeting, I set about making the dinner.

By the time they arrived I was wondering if I could be in early labour, as the backache was coming and going more like contractions than muscle strain. If I could just get them out again; put Cheryl to bed, and have a rest I was sure the pain would settle. After all, I still had ten days to go; and Cheryl was ten days late - if that was anything to go by! The meal went off with pleasant conversation, and the men headed off, completely unaware of my little secret.

Cheryl was a gem that evening, and dozed off on my knee in her soft cuddly pyjamas. Getting her to bed was a little more difficult than usual, with the pain in my back halting the procedure a time or two on the way upstairs. Afterwards, with a mug of tea resting on my bump, I decided it was time to have a little talk to my eagerly awaited son or daughter. "It is time to settle down now," I explained, "Mummy has had a busy day, and you can't possibly come until 'Uncle' Bob leaves in a few days." Thankfully I never had a verbal response to any of my mother/baby conversations; just the occasional kick or somersault! This time the response was a strong tightening of the tummy, accompanied by lower back pain that made me groan. "Don't do this to me, baby. Not yet!" Ten minutes later the performance was repeated, and ten minutes after that again. After a quick trip upstairs to check my pre-prepared hospital bag and to leave Cheryl's clothes ready for the morning, I went into the kitchen to get supper organized.

I heard the men's voices, and quickly flicked on the kettle. "Philip, can you come into the kitchen, please?" I requested. After a peck on the cheek, and before he could launch into his report on a successful meeting, I said, "I think I'm in labour." His response was typical of a man who likes everything to be well organized, and on time: "Don't be silly, you are not due for ten days yet. . . and Bob is here. What can we do with him?"

Needless to say, rearrangements were made, and, five hours later, on the 25th November 1981 at 3.30 in the morning Master Paul Campbell weighed in at 8lb 14oz. He was big, with real boyish features, and a head of dark hair. His wrinkled skin and loud cry made us laugh with joy. He was so beautiful. . .and so perfect! As I held him in my arms my hands glided over his head. Feeling the open soft spots in his skull, just under the skin, reassured me that all was well. "Look at his lovely big head," were the first words I uttered to his dad as I nursed our new little son. The staff threw a knowing glance, realizing the importance of such an unusual comment from a new mother. I thought nothing could compare with giving birth for the first time, but the sense of relief and delight this time round was overwhelming. God was allowing us the same opportunity given to the majority of parents, to have a well, healthy baby. We were in for a real treat, and one we did not take for granted!

Paul charmed everyone who saw him; even Cheryl smiled at the strange new noises in the house. It was not possible for Cheryl to be jealous of her new brother. She didn't know how; and grannies and grandas, aunties and uncles all managed to lavish their attention on both her and the new arrival at the same time. It was really like having two babies at once; only the younger was soon outstripping the older in his ability to do things. Watching the speed of his development was amazing. Things that other parents took for granted filled us with wonder. From the ability to catch hold of his own toes and put them in his mouth….to the dexterity of pinching Cheryl's soother out of her mouth and placing it in his own! Every day was a delight that helped us deal with what was going on in the life of his 'big' sister.

* * *

Three months before Paul was born, Cheryl had started attending Segal House Nursery Unit. The unit is run by the charity organisation Mencap, which provides help for children and adults with learning difficulties, and their families. Segal House was unusual, in that, it provided multidisciplinary care for very young children with varying disabilities, from two years old. Physiotherapy, speech therapy, occupational therapy, and the services of a social worker were all available to the children on site. That meant reducing the number of outpatient clinic appointments, but increasing the actual 'hands on' time with therapists. There were also the classroom staff who cared for the children, and helped stimulate them through play. Added to all this, the family got a well needed break for part of two to three days a week.

That was my special time with Paul; time exclusively for him. Segal House provides a truly wonderful service, greatly appreciated by families.

However, leaving Cheryl there for the first time was rather traumatic. We had come in contact with a few children when waiting for appointments at clinics, but walking into the classroom at Segal House that day was something we were not prepared for. It was a lovely bright room, with nice smells and nursery music playing; but it was the children who took us aback. There were eight to ten severely handicapped toddlers in different positions in the room. Some were lying on mats, others were being held, while a few sat in strange looking chairs. I had never seen so many disabled children all together before. And for the first time I realized that we were not alone. In fact, many families out there faced the same problems we faced day by day. I was just unaware of the size of the problem until that moment.

We really did live in a different world now. Soon we would befriend people whose paths never would have crossed ours, if it had not been for our precious children. At the parent support groups we discussed difficulties, and shared solutions, or at least ideas. Difficulties discussed were as diverse as walking the benefits minefield; to managing your child on public transport. There were also fun nights arranged, combining socializing with fundraising to enable the nursery to continue operating. Laughter was a release, while at other times we shared tears. It was particularly sad to watch some marriages break up because the husband could not cope with the suffering of his child, or with the lack of attention he was receiving. We witnessed human nature at its best, and occasionally at its worst. How it taught me to pray for God's protection over our marriage, and to build a strong relationship with our young son. I vowed he would never become a second class member of our family because of the time that had to be spent with his sister.

The two and a half years Cheryl spent at Segal House Nursery were strangely settled. Apart from the development of epileptic seizures, Cheryl's health was pretty good. A daily routine of physiotherapy was worked into our lives, although it was disappointing to see how little progress was made. Cheryl was lots of work, but no trouble, as she was such a sweet natured child. My parents were a great help with the care of both children, while other family members threw in their lot with the babysitting. Paul brought real happiness into our home, as he continued to delight us every waking moment (well, most of them!). His constant kisses and hugs for Cheryl were not always tolerated by her, even though he meant well! And we always had to keep an eye on his desire to share, especially the sweets he wanted her to taste! For Paul, Cheryl had always been there; and it was not until he was much older that he realised that his sister was quite different to those of his friends.

Cheryl's seizures brought a number of changes. Just how aware she was of what was happening is difficult to measure, but it was disturbing for us to witness. It also brought a concern over why it was happening now after being seizure-free for her first two years. Did it herald some kind of deterioration in her condition? We just did not know. Also regular medication had to be introduced - the first of many, with the dilemma of treatment versus side-effects. The kindly, elderly paediatrician we had so much confidence in, was about to retire, and decided it would be best to pass Cheryl on to the newly appointed paediatric neurologist at the Royal Belfast Hospital for Sick Children.

The first visit was a disaster as far as I was concerned! The new consultant may have been some kind of a medical genius, but that's not what mattered to me. What was important was how she treated my child as a person. Yet she did not touch Cheryl, apart from to do 'medical' things, and she never spoke to her once. Added to which she changed her anti-convulsant medication yet again! How I was going to work with this woman I didn't know, and I definitely didn't want to see her again. But we did have to go back, as we had no choice. The second visit was better, with more interaction with Cheryl, and I could see that she had a genuine concern for all of us. Over the next eighteen years this lady became a big part of our lives. We learned to trust each other with Cheryl's care, and a great respect developed between us. I can honestly say now that I would not have wanted anyone else in the world to have had the medical responsibility of my children. She was an amazing paediatrician; totally devoted to a group of children, who are among the most vulnerable members of our society. I thank God for her, and I am so glad she was on our side!

* * *

Surprisingly enough life became quite routine. Our family may have looked a bit different when we were seen in public, (and we certainly didn't hide away) but this was *our* family, and perfectly normal to us. Being busy with two children meant I tended not to dwell on what I wished for, but got on with what I had. That is, until something or other came along to rock my boat.

For example take the Sunday morning I managed to get out to church, while Philip was away preaching somewhere else. Both Paul and Cheryl were in crèche, and I was settling down to enjoy the sermon. Our minister was a wonderful preacher, and I just soaked up his messages, especially as it was not possible for me to attend all the services anymore. A good way into the sermon he made a statement that made my blood boil. "We have no right to question the things that God brings into our lives," he said, "what He does, He always does for our good."

I have no idea what he said next, because I switched from listening to arguing with him in my head! "How dare you," I fumed silently, with fists clenched and lips pursed. "What right have you to talk about questioning God? You with your perfect little family; your healthy, happy little boy and girl! What do you know about it?" To say I was angry is to understate the mood I was in. I have no idea where it all came from. I had left the house in good form, yet now I was inwardly displaying an anger I did not realize was there. How easy it is to file away in the subconscious, feelings and hurts you decide not to deal with at the time. That day I learned how bitterness can weave its way into your being, and just how destructive it could be if you let it stay.

The sermon continued alongside the battle that was going on inside me. My parents sitting next to me were totally unaware of my anguish. Suddenly I was brought back to the reality of the service by singing. It wasn't the congregation, as I first thought, it was the minister! I had obviously missed the bits where he showed his concern for those who were walking through difficulties; I was too busy waging my own private war with him. But God had broken through to deliver His promise to me yet again.

> "It will be worth it all," he sang, "when we see Jesus,"
> "Life's trials will seem so small, when we see Christ.
> One glimpse of His dear face, all sorrow will erase,
> So bravely run the race, 'til we see Christ."

The words washed over my being; challenging, condemning, and healing. Then the tears came. I heard God say to my heart, "Catherine, I know it is hard. But *one* day it will be worth it all, I promise you. If only you could learn to trust Me. Be brave. Keep on running. I am right there with you." And I was so ashamed. Ashamed of my anger; my bitterness; and my blame. My poor mother sat with me while the rest of the congregation stood to sing the closing hymn. She thought I was crying because of the sermon, but that was only part of the reason for my tears. I was crying because I was sorry for my rage; sorry for allowing a root of bitterness to take hold of me. And I was crying because I didn't deserve God's patience. Yet once again He was displaying His love to me, and covering my life with His promised presence.

'It will be worth it all' written by Esther K. Rusthol

Four
Joy - Given and Taken Away

HERE we were again, at another outpatient clinic in another hospital, only this time I didn't know why we had been sent for. However, the hospital was only at the bottom of our street, and so it didn't take much effort to get there. The words 'Community Paediatric Clinic' were printed at the top of the appointment letter, and an unknown doctor's name typed beside our allocated time slot. I was a little agitated at having to attend, as Cheryl was normally looked after at the 'Children's' in Belfast. After polite introductions, I enquired as to why we had been sent for? It seemed that the local health trust was under some government regulation to see all 'special needs' children in their area, annually. The fact that Cheryl was already five years old and had never been sent for before was lost on them!

Having no access to her present hospital records meant that I had to respond to questions, whose answers would simply be filed away, and would make no difference to her care. In my opinion it was a pointless exercise, but the doctor was pleasant, and we spent some time discussing microcephaly; each learning from the other. During the conversation some mention was made of life-expectancy, and it stopped me in my tracks. Until this point I had never thought about Cheryl's life being shortened. Trying to retain my composure, I questioned the doctor in a casual manner, as I didn't want him to know he was giving me information that I wasn't privy to before. "Is there a generally accepted life-expectancy for microcephaly, then?" I queried. "Children with Cheryl's level of disability rarely see their teens," he replied.

My heart was heavy as I walked the few hundred yards home. I guess that parents don't normally think of their child dying before them; even if that child has major problems. It's just not the thing to talk about; however that night as I lay in my husband's arms we talked for the first time of that awful prospect. The possibility that one day Cheryl might die. It brought things sharply into focus for me. It wasn't something I dwelt on all the time, but it lurked in the back of my mind, surfacing from time to time, especially when Cheryl was ill.

At times I looked at Paul, and dreaded the thought that he might be left an only child. He was such a sociable boy, and, as a toddler now, he had great affection for his sister. Talking from an early age, he would chatter away to her. The fact that her only reply was a smile - and even they were coming less often now - didn't deter this faithful little sibling. Birthdays and Christmas meant that Paul got to open Cheryl's presents as well as his own, and he provided the wind to extinguish the candles on both of their cakes!

"What would you think of us having another baby?" I asked my surprised husband. "Don't you have enough to do!" came an instant reply. The conversation lasted, on and off, for a few days. We covered the subject from all angles ... how would I manage another baby in my already busy schedule? Was the thought of another baby only because we didn't want Paul to be left alone? Was that a good enough reason? What if we had another child with microcephaly? The more we talked about it, the more excited I became at the prospect of another baby; and the less I entertained the notion that anything could possibly go wrong. I was sure Paul would love a sibling to giggle in corners with; someone who could share his secrets, and grow into the future with him.

No one could ever take Cheryl's place in any of our hearts, but the thought of losing her someday helped me decide to try for another baby. Success was only a matter of months away.

The phone rang, and on answering it, I was surprised to hear a midwife introducing herself on the other end of the line. "Mrs. Campbell," she said, "there is a little concern over one of your blood results, and the doctor would like you to come back for another scan." She waited for my response as I tried to steady myself. Thoughts were racing through my mind, not least the fact that microcephaly cannot be detected by blood test. "Which blood tests?" I answered sharply. She was reluctant to tell me, but I persevered until at last she said:"The alpha-fetoprotein is raised . . . but we don't want you to worry until we do further tests."

Stunned, I stood for a minute with my hand covering my mouth. "Spina bifida?" I whispered to myself, "It couldn't be! I can't possibly be having a baby with spina bifida – not when Cheryl has microcephaly!" I gathered myself together, and tried to take a more measured approach. Putting on my midwifery thinking cap, I thought through the situation. "A positive alpha-fetoprotein test is *not* 100% accurate for a diagnosis of spina bifida." The midwife was correct there, and so the best thing to do was not to panic, but to wait for the hospital appointment in a few days time.

The waiting was awful. Only Philip and I knew what was going on; and if I hadn't been so pushy on the phone, neither of us would have had to suffer the accompanying anxiety! We decided not to send unnecessary shock waves into the family until we knew one way or another what was happening.

The day of the scan came. The doctor took a long time moving the device slowly over my slippery tummy. All the while I was praying; my hands cold and clammy with nerves. Occasionally he uttered a few words, the most reassuring being:"The spine looks good to me, I don't know why the tests were reporting high alpha-fetoproteins." I breathed a huge sigh of relief. Yet he continued laboriously moving backwards and forwards with the scanning wand until he exclaimed, "I found the problem!" His loud expression made me jump! "Problem! What problem?" I asked nervously. "I thought you said the spine was okay." The tone of my comments brought him back to the reality of an anxious mother on the couch.

Turning the scan screen towards me, he pointed out a small black bubble. I shrugged my shoulders in his direction, indicating that I hadn't a clue what he was showing me! "This pregnancy started out as a twin pregnancy," he explained, "but only an empty sac formed . . . no second baby. The sac is now being reabsorbed and throwing off proteins in your blood – hence the false test result. Good news all round – this baby is perfectly fine!" The atmosphere in the room changed completely. Furrowed brows became laughter lines, and we set off home relieved and more excited than before, with the words ringing in my ears: "This baby is perfectly fine!"

By the time my tummy was getting too large to pass off as overeating to an astute three year old, we told Paul the news that he was going to have a baby brother or sister. He danced around the living room, whooping with glee and causing Cheryl to wriggle with all the excitement. I'm glad we decided to hold off telling him until then because the remaining weeks were filled with one question after another! (All answered, I might say, with simplicity – only giving enough information to satisfy curiosity!) A short stay in hospital for ENT surgery dampened Paul's fervour, but it quickly returned.

My last scan was just four weeks before my due-date, and the obstetrician's enthusiastic report continued in the same vein as all the previous ones. "Home in a boat, Mrs. Campbell," he said as he wiped the gel off my *huge* abdomen, "there's nothing wrong with this baby!"

Just three weeks later he was on duty when I was admitted to the labour ward, and I was glad. He wasn't just a good doctor, he was fun as well. We were sure of a few laughs to break the somewhat tense atmosphere that can surround the 'labour' experience. The first laugh wasn't long in coming. It was Sunday morning and Philip was due to preach at a service in Belfast. He wondered if he would have time to go and preach, and still be back for the delivery. He shared his dilemma with the doctor, who gawped at him incredulously. "Tell them to sing another hymn!" he replied. "It'll probably do them more good than one of your sermons! This baby will be here before you would get a chance to step into the pulpit!"

He was exactly right! Our beautiful little girl was born at 11.40am on Sunday the 28th of July 1985, right in the middle of church service time! She was 1lb 7oz lighter than her brother, and even with her screwed-up face and wrinkled skin she was just a little dream. Another girl, I could hardly believe it! This time she was handed to Philip first, who was simply beside himself with delight. He kept kissing her sticky little forehead, while from the corner of the room came the retort: "I told you they should sing another hymn!"

She was all wrapped up in green towels to keep her warm when Philip put her in my arms. Her face looked so tiny, and her hands felt satin soft as I put them to my lips to kiss them. "Welcome Little One," was all I could say. She took my breath away!

Philip was packed off home to announce the good news, which all of Newtownabbey seemed to know before he reached there. (My sister had been standing outside our home church telling everyone about the baby as the service ended!) I think invisible fireworks filled the sky; people were so delighted for us!

Back in the hospital I found myself alone for the first time with Joy. (What else could we have called her?!) I talked quietly to her as she cradled in my arms. "Let's have a closer look at you, Little One," I said, bending down to kiss her. "I haven't seen your toes yet — you're so well wrapped up." As I loosened the wrap my heart skipped a beat, and a quiet gasp slipped out — her head looked much smaller than Paul's had, three years earlier. My hands gently moved around her skull, feeling for the soft spots that should be quite large at this stage. The one at the front was there, but small — and panic started to set in as I couldn't find the one at the back! Then it hit me. She looked so like her sister — so like Cheryl!

I wrapped her up again — afraid to think; afraid to ask anyone to look at her. "But the midwife did check her out," I reminded myself, "therefore she must be okay." I played mental ping pong; torturing myself one minute and reassuring myself the next. To and fro I went, convincing myself she was microcephalic — so like her sister; then reminding myself of all the antenatal tests that had said she was perfect. The very doctor who was at her birth had said just three weeks earlier: "There's nothing wrong with this baby!" I was frantic. "Please God…please take away this awful fear, and give me Your peace," I pleaded. "Everyone at home will be so excited right now – I can't tell them how I feel," I convinced myself. "Of course she is like her sister. Lots of sisters look alike." I was trying to replace panic with persuasion; reminding myself that Paul had been a sturdy big boy, while Joy was a fine little girl! Today was to be a day of celebration, and no silly thoughts from an over-anxious mother were going to spoil it! So, strong-willed as I was, I determined not to say anything to anyone about my concerns until Philip and I were alone that night, during fathers' visiting time.

The baby and I were moved to the ward before visiting time. It was frantic! The excitement was palpable with grandparents and aunties cooing and fussing over the new addition! The fact that she was a girl seemed to add to their delight, and joining in their happiness settled my heart. "New mothers are notoriously emotional," I thought, "everything is fine – I am sure God wouldn't do this to us again." After they left, I settled down to feed Joy. This time as I held her my feelings were only those of happiness, accompanied by the thrill I had denied myself only a few hours earlier. "Your mummy is a silly woman," I said to Joy as I put her back in her little perspex cot. Looking at her sleeping through the clear plastic I settled down, both in heart and body, for a rest.

Philip arrived that evening, having had an afternoon sleep, looking more human but just as chuffed to see his new daughter again. I let him tell me about all the phone calls he had made and the responding delight they had brought. He explained how Paul was a bit miffed that he was going to have to wait until the next day to see his new sister - but calmed by the fact that he and granny would come alone and not have to share the baby with anyone else! Cheryl had just smiled, probably more in response to being spoken to, rather than to the news she was given. It was only five days until her sixth birthday, and I wondered how she would respond to the feeling of a wriggly baby in her arms once again!

Philip looked the picture of contentment while cradling Joy in his arms on the armchair beside my bed. I felt guilty at disturbing him by mentioning my earlier fears. But we had worked at having a marriage that avoided secrets; and so I gently told him of my panic in the labour ward, and concerns over the size of the baby's head. I could see both shock and disbelief cross his face at the same time. Initially he said nothing, while I felt a few little tears trickle down my cheeks. Wiping them off quickly, I watched Philip change the baby's position in his arms so that he could get a good look at her. "Her head is smaller than Paul's," he sighed, "but she is smaller all over than Paul. I really don't think you should worry . . . she's beautiful." His comments made sense, and I promised I would ask the paediatrician about it when he visited the ward the next day.

It was nearly three o'clock and I was getting so excited about introducing Paul to his new little sister. He burst in through the door, pulling granny behind him, and ran straight past me to the cot. With a flurry of activity he swung a tiny little pink bag into the cot shouting: "This is for you Baby." And in the same breath he turned to me and asked, "What do you call it?" Explaining that the 'it' was a 'she', and that her name was Joy, I lifted my excited pre-schooler into my arms. He went on to tell me that he had taken money out of his piggy bank, and had picked her present all by himself! "Do you like them?" he exclaimed to Joy, as he pulled a tiny little pair of lacy pink and white socks out of the bag. His loud voice made her wriggle, much to his delight. "Let's try on her socks, Mummy," he said; at the same time pulling the blanket from around her. Granny took control, lifting Paul up on the bed beside me, and then placing Joy carefully in his arms. He held her so cautiously, almost afraid to move and biting his bottom lip in deep concentration. Granny tried on the socks, and we all laughed! "They're too big Mummy!" he shouted in disappointment. "Just you wait Paul," interrupted Granny, "I bet they'll fit her by next week!"

It was a lovely visit. As Paul turned to go he kissed Joy on the cheek, "I love you, sister," he said, "and I'm going to tell Cheryl all about you!" Little did that baby know then just how precious she would become to her big brother, and just how protective his love for her would be.

* * *

The following day I returned from lunch in the day-room to meet the 'baby doctor' coming out of my room. "Just checked your baby," he said, "she's ready for home." Blocking his exit I surprised him by asking, "What do you think about the size of her head?" He quickly looked at Joy's medical notes, trying to establish his authority in this uneasy situation. (The doctors who carried out the baby discharge examinations were usually the most junior on the paediatric rota, and they were not often asked difficult questions by mothers!) "Her head?" he stammered. "What's wrong with her head?" Guiding him back towards the cot, I replied:"Don't you think it's a bit small in comparison with her length and weight?" Glancing at the measurements he had taken, he became very defensive. "It's on the lower limits of normal…but I'm not concerned," he blustered. "You nurses are always looking for problems. Why don't you just take this baby home and enjoy her!" "But I already have one child at home with microcephaly – I don't think it is unreasonable for me to be concerned!"

My last comment had totally un-nerved him. It was obvious that he had not bothered to check if there had been any antenatal concerns about this baby, making him totally unprepared for postnatal queries! He did not like my challenge, and continued commenting on fussy mothers who imagined problems as he made his withdrawal.

The fact that I had dared to question him was obviously reported to the midwife, and I felt like a naughty child when she appeared in my room. I needn't have, as she quietly sat beside me and asked what I was worried about. She listened carefully and took Joy out of my arms, running her hand over Joy's skull. "Her head circumference is still within normal limits, Catherine," she said kindly,"and if you are still worried in a few weeks time take her to your own doctor." I felt as if I had done battle and couldn't wait to phone Philip to tell him that we were ready for home. "Maybe the doctor was right," I said to myself,"maybe I am creating problems where there are none!"

* * *

Paul's excitement more than made up for any lack of it in Cheryl as her sixth birthday dawned the day after Joy and I arrived home. Philip, delighted to have all his family back home, managed some party shopping, while granny and I handled the table and cooking. By the time our living room was filled with party-goers Cheryl was all dressed up in her lovely birthday frock, adorned by the big 'I am six' badge picked by her brother! She was in great form, and didn't seem bothered by the new noises in the house, coming from her little sister. As I looked around the room I couldn't help but feel so privileged that my children were born into an extended family who loved each one of them so very much. We were blessed indeed! Cheryl, who was small and slight for her age, cuddled up to her granda and I don't know which of them had the bigger smile. I was glad she smiled today as there were more and more days when she didn't, or perhaps couldn't. This would be a birthday we would remember for many happy reasons.

Joy, like her sister and brother before her, had an unsettled time with colic every evening. Apart from that she was a very good baby, feeding and sleeping well. It was during her waking moments that my concerns continued about her head size and poor muscle tone. She was still very young, but her floppiness was causing me anxiety. I took it upon myself to contact the physio from Segal House, with whom we had remained friendly after Cheryl had left to go to Hillcroft Special School.

At almost six weeks old, Joy was put through her paces by our friend. Reflexes and responses were checked, and Joy was encouraged to perform like any other six week old baby. I could see as time went on that she wasn't doing very well. "She's beautiful, Catherine," the physio said. I could feel a 'but' coming on, and I was right. "I think it might be a good idea to let Cheryl's paediatrician see her … just to check her out." She went on to explain her concerns, promising that she would try to speak to the paediatrician before I phoned her secretary the next day.

I felt like a lump of clay driving home – emotionless, empty, and unwilling to accept what had been *my* concerns in the first place. Philip reacted more positively about the advice to get a paediatrician's opinion. "Maybe this will settle your mind once and for all that everything is alright. I think it's a good idea," he said.

Three days later I was sitting in the waiting room of the busy paediatric neurology clinic, with Joy on my knee. Never before had a hospital appointment come so quickly. Our friend, the physio, obviously had some clout with the paediatrician!

Introductions were not needed as this was the doctor who saw Cheryl every 3 -6 months. She did however speak to the very little patient in front of her, and stroked her cheek. (What a difference there was in the past four years!)

Quickly repeating the various tests carried out a few days before, she handed Joy back to me to dress. I didn't want to speak, which was unusual for me, so she spoke first: "We'll talk after you come back from X-ray," she said. "I've asked one of the radiologists to do an ultrasound of the ventricles in Joy's brain, and he has kindly agreed to do it today." I'm sure I looked surprised as she handed me the form. It usually took a few weeks to arrange such a test, so I meekly said, "Thanks", and headed off to X-ray.

Some time later, Joy and I sat in front of the doctor again. How I wished Cheryl hadn't been sick that day! If she had been able to go to school then Philip would have been here with me - I felt very alone and vulnerable. The doctor's first words caused me to gasp; "I'm sorry," she said. How could two such small words reveal so much! "The tests and ultrasound have shown that Joy's brain has stopped growing. She has microcephaly – just like her sister," she went on to say. Joy started to cry, and I realized it wasn't only my breath I was holding tightly. Loosening my grip slightly on Joy allowed a restrained sob to escape from my lips. Before I could reach for my handbag, the doctor had landed a pile of hankies on my knee. The tears came, but no words – I couldn't speak – I just wanted to go home. I *needed* to go home!

I remember leaving the hospital, and I remember arriving at my front door, but I don't remember how I got there! There was obviously a myriad of guardian angels protecting us that afternoon! Thankfully, Paul was at his friend's house when his distraught mother arrived home that afternoon, and Cheryl's high temperature kept her asleep.

Philip took Joy out of my arms, as I stumbled through the events of the day, weeping. I felt so cruel telling my lovely husband that his darling little Joy was going to end up like his beloved Cheryl – never able to walk, or talk; never able to sing or play; never able to plant a kisses on our cheeks or call our names! The pain was unbearable, and tears flowed in the darkness that surrounded us in that moment.

A few hours later, after composing ourselves a little we took the girls with us to break the awful news to both sets of parents. Paul stayed at his friends for tea, and we decided not to tell him for a while yet that his precious baby sister was handicapped. We wanted him to enjoy her as a baby, first and foremost. Having the girls with us gave the grandparents something to do with their arms, while they listened to news that broke their hearts once again. They grieved not only for their grandchildren, but also for their own children, who were hurting so much.

News spread like wildfire, and we were surrounded by an outpouring of love and attention from friends and neighbours, as well as family. Apart from the odd comment of: "It's a pity they didn't content themselves with the two children they already had," we were overwhelmed by kindness. So much kindness in fact, that I was afraid Paul would know that something was up, what with lots of visitors and frequent whispering! I didn't want him to be disappointed with Joy, you see. He just loved being with her and I didn't want that to change.

A few days later Paul was on the floor drawing a picture, when, without even lifting his head he said matter-of-factly: "Mummy. Is Joy handicapped – like Cheryl?" I nearly dropped! Panic set in, and I started to stammer. "Would you still love her if she was handicapped?" I asked foolishly, not knowing what to say. Paul tutted in response, still concentrating on his picture: "'Course I would . . . silly Mummy!" Oh, how badly I had underestimated the loyalty of this nearly-four year old. Calling him to me, I sat him on my knee and told him that, "Yes, Joy is handicapped – but we will keep on loving her just as much as we love Cheryl." "I'll give her my picture, Mummy," he replied, and he jumped off my knee, unperturbed, to finish his masterpiece!

* * *

My rainbow seemed to be dissipating. God had promised me six years earlier that He would be with me through every storm and cloud. Now, however, I couldn't sense His presence at all – there was just enormous disappointment and sadness. For six years I had experienced His help - for six years I had rested in the knowledge that God knew what He was doing. I had learnt so much over that time from His word, and could say that I had been to places with God that I had never dreamed possible. I was a spiritually different person than I had been before Cheryl was born. Yet for the first time since then I felt unsure of His love. My heart was empty, and my mind was exhausted from trying to work out what good could possibly come out of all this. "Have I not learned enough, Lord?" was my cry of despair.

Day seemed to follow day with no break in the darkness. I functioned at the level of necessity, while trying to avoid being in public if I could help it. Tears let me down too easily, and I didn't want to disappoint others with my feelings of disappointment with God.

Having watched Cheryl's condition deteriorate over the years, I knew exactly what to expect for Joy. That was the heartbreaking part – I knew *exactly* how badly handicapped she would be. With Cheryl we didn't know what was around the corner, and that protected us in some way. But with Joy we already knew the road she was about to take, and it was hard to look at this little baby and know what lay ahead for her. It just didn't seem fair. In time I would understand that God didn't promise to be fair as we understand it – He promised to be right. Determining fairness requires the ability to see both sides of the situation, and with 'eternal things' that won't be possible until we reach Heaven. What is required for now is trust.

One thing I did learn over those years was not to neglect the bible, because this is how God speaks to us. Closing the bible is like refusing to allow God to speak. I desperately needed to hear Him speak into my encircling gloom. It is hard to concentrate though when you are emotionally low, so I was reading from a book of daily readings at the time. Only one small verse for each day was required reading, with the accompanying 'thought' given by the author.

Only five weeks after the news of Joy's diagnosis I read these words from 1 Peter 1:6b - 8a: "You have been grieved by various trials, that the genuineness of your faith, being much more precious than gold that perishes, though it is tested by fire, may be found to praise, honour, and glory at the revelation of Jesus Christ, whom having not seen you love." That day's 'thought' went on to talk about a customer asking the owner of a china shop why one set of china had a design on it that stood out clearly more distinct than all the rest. The explanation given was that it had more work done on it – it was put through the fire twice in order that the design would shine like gold!

I gasped as I read the words – 'through the fire twice', and recognized that God was speaking directly into my life once more. And in the darkness of my sadness I could see something glimmer…the faint colours of a rainbow – the return of God's promised presence. "Catherine, can you trust Me with the things you can't understand?" He whispered to my heart. "Will you allow Me to work on you, in order that My glory might be seen?" A realization that I was only experiencing the earthly part of the story helped me to respond, "Yes, Lord. But only if You don't leave me to walk alone!"

The colour of the rainbow brightened in my heart, as I remembered that this promise had already been given.

Five

Angels Unawares

LIFE was very busy with three children – two of whom required everything to be done for them. In reality it was more than everything, as physiotherapy (and lots of other 'therapies') had to be added to the mix. Then include hospital visits, clinic appointments plus other sundries, such as fittings for wheelchairs and buggies. Oh, and not forgetting all the extra professionals who visited our home. Remember also the fact that there was no such thing as a full night's sleep – ever! – and I think you might just begin to understand what I mean by busy!

Paul was enjoying being a 'big boy' and heading off to school every day, usually about thirty minutes before the school bus rolled down the street for Cheryl. I doubt whether there were any mornings when I got off that particular bus, after securing Cheryl into her seat, without a smile on my face. Special needs children are notoriously welcoming and good natured. So we were always greeted with 'Hellos' from those who could speak, and happy noises from those who couldn't! Sometimes we had to examine new toys, or hear the latest news from the happy passengers – especially after Christmas or birthdays! It's a wonder that the bus ever arrived at school on time! Still, we learnt so much from these wonderful children about the simple things of life. Their ability to be happy and content with what we would regard as very little, always astounded me.

School for Cheryl was not books and blackboards, but rather a home from home place where she received care and stimulation. Large colourful paintings, usually displaying seasonal scenes, covered the walls of her classroom. Sensory equipment and toys stood to attention waiting to be brought to life by eight little pairs of hands. Beautiful, relaxing smells greeted those who entered; while cots and soft mats revealed the need of rest for their frail pupils. Success in education for Cheryl and her classmates was responding appropriately to touch, sound, or visual objects in whatever programme was being used. The staff had amazing patience; even love for the children. Cheryl's teacher reported on the class activities in her home/school diary so that we knew what had taken place each day. A record of any seizures, and how well she ate, along with any other delights or disasters were recorded to fill the gap in our knowledge that Cheryl was unable to fill herself. And so we could chat to her about school, and the staff could talk to her about home with the information we gave them in return. All of this made school a very special place for all of us. In addition, the open visiting policy in Cheryl's room was of great help to those parents who felt uneasy about leaving their profoundly disabled child in someone else's care.

While Cheryl and Paul were at school I enjoyed special time with Joy (and the housework)! It is important that each child is treated as an individual and we tried, where possible, to interact personally with each one every day. I had heard it said that 'normal' siblings can often feel neglected in a family that has a child with special needs. That I find hard to understand as Paul was such a blessing in our lives, and watching him grow helped us enjoy the true delights of childhood. From his earliest years he and his dad had a day or afternoon out together every week – just the two of them. Mummy wasn't even told where they were going – it was their secret until they returned! Sometimes it was something as simple as a trip to the park, or the swimming pool – occasionally a ride on a train, or a visit to the cinema. They even went on 'Captain Planet' patrol, collecting discarded cans, and exchanging them for pocket money! Mind you, their excursions usually included an ice–cream, or drink and a doughnut afterwards!! That continued for years, and I don't know who enjoyed their time together more – father or son? Time with our children is always the best thing we can put into their lives, and giving time to Paul was no chore.

And so life continued on at a 'normal- for- us' pace after Joy's diagnosis. Cheryl had remained small for her age, but I became concerned with the increasing episodes of vomiting that seemed to blight most of her days. She was losing weight and feeding her was taking longer, with less enjoyment on her part. And so, for the first time since her hip surgery, Cheryl was admitted to hospital for investigation of the problem.

It was a Saturday morning. Philip was away in Scotland preaching, and Granda was holding the fort at home with Joy and Paul while Granny and I visited Cheryl. While we were chatting with the staff nurse, and explaining that I would return after breast-feeding Joy; I noticed something alarming out of the corner of my eye. Cheryl, who had been previously restful, suddenly lurched forward and then fell back into the pillow. Her breathing was noisy and fast, and her pale cheeks had turned grey. Something was badly wrong! The staff nurse turned on her heels to get a doctor, while I ran to Cheryl. She was clearly unconscious, and unable to respond to her pleading mummy's voice! My organized nurse's mindset helped to keep me outwardly calm, while inside I was panicking. At least the outward veneer meant that they allowed me to stay with Cheryl while the medical team swung into action. In a short time oxygen was administered; monitors were in place, and an IV canula was put into her arm ready for whatever drugs they felt Cheryl needed. Unfortunately – they didn't know what the trouble was – so a more senior doctor was sent for!

This time I was not allowed to stay while Cheryl was examined. That gave me time to speak to my mum, who was great at taking control when things went wrong. We were just in the process of agreeing to Joy's first ever bottle feed, when the doctor interrupted our conversion. "I think you need to get your husband here as quickly as possible," she said. I tried to explain to her that he was in Scotland, but she just interjected with: "It doesn't matter where he is; you need to get him home. Cheryl is very sick." I stood there stunned, and could feel my mother gently rubbing my back, just like she did when I was little. The doctor continued, now that she had my undivided attention. "I think Cheryl is in 'status'." She explained that a continuous epileptic seizure was in progress, and that it was preventing Cheryl from regaining consciousness. "We have no idea if or when it will stop – it's continuing in spite of the drugs we've given to her."

Mum was next to speak: "I'll go home and get in touch with Philip, and bottle feed Joy. You are needed here with Cheryl. Soon people will be praying, Love - try not to worry." My bottom lip trembled as my own mother took me in her arms, and I tried to hold back the tears to avoid upsetting her further. She nipped in behind the bed screens to kiss her darling granddaughter goodbye – unsure of whether she would see her again. With the sound of her footsteps rushing up the corridor, I went to sit with Cheryl. Even my tears dripping on her face didn't make her stir. "Surely she can't be so sick," I thought. "Your daddy will be in such a panic Cheryl," I whispered to her, and my thoughts went out to him receiving the news and trying to arrange travel home quickly. "Oh God," I prayed, "please let him get home in time."

It was only after the staff had finished working with Cheryl for a little while that I was suddenly stopped in my tracks with a disturbing thought. It was Saturday afternoon, and Philip had told me that the evangelism team were hoping to get the chance to go to see one of the big Scottish football league matches, while they were over there. This was before the time of mobile phones – "How on earth would Mum be able to get in touch with him?" But God knew that Cheryl and I needed Philip, and He was working out His own plan. When I phoned Mum later, she told me that she was only through the front door when the phone rang – it was Philip! He was ringing to see how everyone was before he went to the football match! But the poor guy was given the news that he had to come home straight away. It was one of the worst days in his life, as he tried to get a flight arranged – there were no seats available from Edinburgh or Glasgow! In the end a friend had to drive him all the way from Edinburgh to Stranraer to catch a ferry! That man was the first of our ministering angels that day.

Every minute seemed like an hour. There was no change in Cheryl's condition, and all we could do was wait! Inactive waiting causes the mind to wander, and rarely does it wander into good territory. The futile 'what ifs' came with force … destroying peace and heightening a sense of hopeless anxiety. 'What if' … Cheryl didn't recover? 'What if' … she died before her daddy got home? 'What if' … she does recover and is left worse than before? 'What if'? On and on it went, until my 'what ifs' became completely ridiculous! Those two little words are undoubtedly the devil's torment of the soul! Resting my elbows on the bed, I covered my head with my hands in despair and didn't hear anyone approach. I jumped when I felt a hand gently touch my shoulder, and looking up I saw my minister. The poor man arrived in the middle of my darkest point, as I was drowning in 'what ifs'! I have no doubt that God had sent him, because I needed his quiet, gentle counsel at that time.

He sat at the other side of Cheryl's cot, holding her hand tenderly. After a while, and sensing that there was more going on in my heart than Cheryl's medical emergency he asked: "So what is really worrying you Catherine?" Oh, how glad I was that he asked that particular question! "Will Cheryl go to Heaven if she dies?" I blurted out. Stammering I went on to explain that Cheryl didn't have the capacity to understand about sin and salvation – and I was afraid. "What will happen to her?" I repeated. He barely flinched, but in his soft Welsh accent he gently rebuked me: "Ah Catherine," his voice lilted, "do you not know your God?" "Of course she will be in Heaven, for Jesus Himself said: 'Blessed are the pure in heart, for they shall see God'." He then reached into his pocket and pulled out his bible. For the next little while we looked together at the story of the death of King David's baby son, and he read David's words to me from 2 Samuel 12:23: "I shall go to him, but he shall not return to me."

He looked at me firmly and said words that I shall never forget: "If Cheryl dies she will go to Heaven, because Jesus said the pure in heart will see God – and one day you will go to her, just as we have been reading." The issue was settled once and for all in my heart; even on that darkest of days God was willing to minister peace through His servant. Deep down I had always known this to be true, but I didn't know where to look for the biblical evidence that brought the *absolute* assurance that I needed.

The time passed and my minister sat with me – mostly in silence. I was so glad that I didn't have to be alone, in spite of the fact that the staff were constantly checking on Cheryl's condition. And I knew it would take time for other family members to reach me.

Suddenly I heard a baby cry in the distance – "I know that cry," I said, as my best friend turned into the ward carrying a fretful Joy. "She doesn't like the bottle! She has decided only her mummy will do!" my friend exclaimed as I gave her a hug. The minister retreated while my friend deposited Joy into my arms. The sound of my voice calmed her for a few minutes as we quickly exchanged information on what was happening at home and with Cheryl. Soon Joy was happily feeding with only the shaking of her remaining sobs interrupting the scene. As she fed I learned that Philip was on his way to Stranraer to catch the ferry, and that Granny was contacting everyone for prayer.

As Joy's 'ministering angel' was putting on her coat to whisk her back home to granny she informed me that another friend was organizing a rota. "What kind of a rota?" I quizzed her. "We are all going to take it in turns to bring Joy in for her feeds every four hours, until this emergency is over! We don't want the wee mite miserable now, do we?" I was so humbled by the love and support given to me by such a great group of friends – most of whom were busy with babies of their own to look after.

Thereafter for the next few days, every four hours, Joy was brought to the ward for a feed and a cuddle, and then taken away again – happy and content. I did feel sorry for whoever was doing the late and early morning feeds though! During the night Granny persevered with the bottle, whether Joy liked it or not! The staff affectionately called the service 'meals on wheels'! And they had an early introduction to a child they would get to know well in the future.

Cheryl remained unconscious until literally ten minutes before her daddy arrived from the boat! She just wakened up - her breathing settled, and all her vital signs returned to normal. The doctor was checking her out when a very stressed and exhausted Philip entered the ward late that night! I rushed to meet him while the doctor explained: "The worst is over, but she's not out of the woods yet." Directing her comments to Philip she went on to say, "I'm sorry we had you rushing all over the country, but we didn't know which way this was going to turn out." He was only half listening as he leaned over the cot to kiss his darling daughter. "Oh Cheryl – you have no idea how glad I am to see you, Sweetheart." Relief at seeing her alive erased the stress lines that had been imprinted on his face during the long journey home.

Soon Cheryl was in a settled sleep, and Philip and I talked quietly into the night, filling in the missing details of the day for each other. Over the next couple of days Cheryl had a few frightening relapses, but once she was stable enough we were able to take her home. How unprepared we were then for the many times we would find ourselves in the same position . . . with Cheryl fighting for her life! And each time we would discover more about true love and friendship, as family and friends pulled out all the stops to help us again and again.

* * *

The bible has plenty to say about 'angels'. Way back in the book of Genesis, Abraham had a visit from three men. They turned out to be 'angels' – sent by God with a special message for Abraham and Sarah. That message was to change the lives of the recipients. In 1 Kings 19 Elijah was in a state of despair when he was visited by an 'angel', who ministered to him in the most practical of ways, by providing food for him and encouraging him to rest. In Hebrews 13 the writer reminds us that those who cross our paths may be 'angels unawares'. In other words we may not recognize them as such, but they are in fact 'messengers from God' sent to meet our needs. God has different ways of showing us that He loves us and that He hears our cries for help. I believe one of those ways is by turning family and friends into 'angels unawares'.

Often God uses them to bring us a message from Himself – usually of love, comfort and concern. At other times it is like the 'angel' who visited Elijah – to bring practical help and meet a present need. Whatever the task, be it only once or over a long period of time, these people are 'angels unawares' – just like the man who drove Philip to the boat, and the girls who operated Joy's 'meals on wheels' service!

Throughout the many crises over many years I have been the beneficiary of countless 'ministering angels'. Sometimes a bunch of flowers lay on the doorstep awaiting my return from hospital - simply saying: "Praying for you". Meals were made; ironing lovingly smoothed; children babysat; school runs undertaken; carpets vacuumed; shopping provided and even *dirty* clothes taken away to be washed! At times I was overwhelmed by the selfless actions of those who loved our family – like the time a group of friends planned for me to visit the hairdressers; all paid for by them. They had arranged the appointment, transport, babysitting – and when I returned they even had my ironing done! And all because they knew I needed a break!

You may be thinking I have quite a group of friends – well I have, but I have also learned how important it is to accept help when it's offered! Many of us turn away 'ministering angels' because we don't want it to appear that we can't manage by ourselves. Pride refuses the answers to our prayers, and then blames God for the burden we 'think' we must carry alone. We not only stop God blessing our lives; we stop God blessing the lives of those who are responding to God's request to act as His messenger.

* * *

But friends weren't only used by God for the very helpful, practical tasks that made our life so much easier. They became vital for our spiritual wellbeing also.

In times of crisis I would frequently have felt physically exhausted, and emotionally low. Often this was brought about purely by the enormity of the situations we had to face. Concentration was, at times, difficult. Reading could only be done in short snippets (as previously explained), while praying was sometimes beyond my emotional capability. There were days when I just didn't know what to pray for any more. Was it right to constantly ask God to bring Cheryl out of some crisis – just to face another one a short time later? What should I pray for concerning Joy? At times it was all too much!

On one such occasion I was speaking to a friend on the parents' phone, in the ward. "I just don't know what to pray for any more," I said to her, after explaining the seriousness of Cheryl's current illness. Her answer still pulls at my heart strings! "Let me do the praying," she said tenderly. "Concentrate your energy on being her mummy." And she wasn't the only one – people all over the UK, and friends throughout the world, wrapped us in their prayers during the times when we felt too weary to pray for ourselves. We didn't only know it as fact; we actually experienced it as we sensed the presence of God creep into Cheryl's ward when all other hope was gone.

It reminded me of the story of when the Old Testament prophet Elijah was faced with the distraught widow, whose son had just died. "Give me your son," said the prophet to the weeping mother – and he took the boy and laid him out before the Lord, and God miraculously answered his prayer and restored the boy to life. There are no greater words that we can say to any distraught parent, whatever the cause of their distress, than those words: "Give me your child." "Let me bring them to the Lord on your behalf." This weary mother allowed others to 'spiritually' lift Cheryl out of my arms at times – and take her to the Lord!

Friendship is undoubtedly one of life's greatest gifts, and I know for sure that some of my friends are 'angels unawares'.

Six
Riding the Roller-Coaster

THE surgical ward was unfamiliar territory for us all. Cheryl was normally nursed in the medical ward, where we knew the staff well – and they knew us. I felt insecure; unsure of how the staff would cope with a child with such diverse needs as Cheryl. Most of their little patients were 'normal' children, in hospital for a variety of surgical procedures. The surgical consultant was the only one known to us, as we had met him at the outpatient clinic. As a nurse I understood both the benefits and the drawbacks of treating patients in specific specialist units. It meant that the best possible care could be given for a particular condition, with the staff very knowledgeable in one area of expertise. Problems arose when you had a patient with complex, multiple needs – the majority of which you had no expertise in . . . like Cheryl! There was also an increased risk of mistakes, especially if you didn't know the child – and the child had no way of communicating with you. For our peace of mind the only solution was to make sure that some of the family were with Cheryl at all times.

Cheryl's vomiting problem was seen as the cause of her earlier crisis. Her anti – epilepsy drugs required to be maintained at a certain level, in order to work effectively. But Cheryl was unable to keep them down, which meant that the drug level dropped causing life - threatening seizures. Drastic measures were required, as it was discovered that a large hiatus hernia was at the root of the problem. Surgical intervention was arranged — hence our admission to this unfamiliar ward.

Cheryl duly went off to theatre, and after what to us was an agonizing wait, she returned to the ward. The staff did their best, and were not unfriendly, but the whole atmosphere made it an unsettling time for us all. The ward was frenetically busy — and so noisy! Not only was it not conducive to recovery, but the frequent, sudden noises startled Cheryl — making her jump! The jumping exacerbated the pain in her large tummy wound as she had no way of protecting herself from it. She couldn't hold her tummy when she went to cough, or tell you when she felt nauseous — the whole experience made her miserable. It was hard to watch! As soon as I could persuade the doctors, we took her home. At least there she was able to rest quietly, and we were hopeful that the surgery would improve her general health significantly.

Once recovered from the actual surgery, Cheryl improved for a short time — but not as much as we had hoped. Feeding her was, at times, a long drawn out process, as the surgery had made swallowing more difficult. Often the 'cure' swapped one set of problems for another! The writhing muscle disorder (athetosis), that accompanied microcephaly, was not only responsible for many of her disabilities, it was also the undoing of her surgical procedures too. The hip that had been repaired when she was thirteen months old was now permanently dislocated by those dysfunctioning muscles (mercifully it was not painful!). That in turn caused her spine to twist - which led to chest deformity - which led to breathing problems. About a year after her surgery and before her eighth birthday, the work carried out on her stomach started to loosen. There were times when we felt guilty at putting Cheryl through so much surgery, yet because we wanted to make her life as comfortable as possible we took some risks. I guess we would also have felt guilty if we hadn't allowed the operations to go ahead, but it did help us to be more cautious when surgery was mentioned for Joy.

So we entered a phase when Cheryl was not only a handicapped child, but often an ill child as well. We tried to keep her days as normal as possible;

sending her to school when she was well enough, and involving her in most of the family activities whenever they came around. There were always plenty of people to give both her and Joy cuddles at the various birthday 'dos', and Christmas celebrations. We took delight in the things many other families took for granted. It was always worth the effort, even when it came to transporting all the special equipment necessary for both of the girls!

Special trips to see friends, usually in the summer, became real treats. Close friends of ours lived on the Ards Peninsula, and we had many happy days with them while both sets of children were small. Paul particularly enjoyed having friends to play with, and usually prepared for our trips to the country a few days in advance! He was always a performer, and while his sisters enjoyed his piano playing and storytelling, they couldn't enter into his desire to put on 'shows'! So you can imagine his delight when he had *five* other budding performers to work with, and a big house and garden to stage the show in! It was great for us parents too, as we were left in peace to enjoy each others' company while rehearsals went on!

Tickets were designed, props painted, and costumes secreted from wardrobes all over the house. Then the show was introduced with great excitement and fanfare: "Ladies and gentlemen!" were the words shouted down cardboard loud-hailers. "Come and see the greatest show on earth!" The children's giggles were stifled by a stern look from Paul, who at seven was the oldest, and took it all very seriously. Once our tickets had been collected, the four of us, along with Cheryl and Joy, were shown to our seats and the show began. We may have been a small audience, but we were very appreciative; clapping and cheering in all the right places! The 'Cloughey Circus' had acrobatic acts, singers, and even magic tricks performed by a magician in a black cape! You can guess that it didn't take much rocking to get the children to sleep that night! It was only one of many such fun–filled days that we enjoyed with different friends, and their families. Their children always treated the girls with tenderness and understanding. One such little boy insisted on holding Cheryl's feeding bowl while I fed her – even though a table was available! He was very patient, as it could take forty five minutes to empty the bowl! But it was his way of helping Cheryl.

There were many such precious memories for us to hide away in our hearts. Times that make us smile, even today.

***

The day both Cheryl and Joy were admitted to hospital *together* felt really strange. Cheryl was seven years old, while Joy was one. In fact neither of them was ill, but both of them were to have brain scans carried out, and so the doctor decided to 'kill two birds with the same stone', metaphorically speaking. It was only an overnight stay, and the staff suggested that Philip and I take advantage of the situation and have a night out together – with the promise that they would look after the girls well. Since we're into metaphors – 'we didn't look a gift horse in the mouth', and enjoyed a nice evening out without the pressure of rushing home.

While we were blessed with selfless babysitters, their number decreased as Cheryl became weaker. So the lot often fell on my parents, without whom it would have been virtually impossible for the two of us to be out of the house at the same time. They carried out tasks that many grandparents would have cringed at – and without a word of complaint. Our love and admiration for them knows no bounds!

We were unsure of what to expect when we attended Outpatients for the scan results. The consultant had both scans clipped to the x-ray box when we entered the room. "It's remarkable," she said, nodding her head, while we took our seats. "It's quite remarkable," she repeated. I became impatient: "What's remarkable?" I questioned. "You would think both of these scans were of the same brain," she replied, "except that the name is different on each of the films. This one is Cheryl's, and this one is Joy's," she said as she pointed. We listened carefully as she tried to explain the complicated films. Even as a nurse I recognised that I was out of my depth with this.

Although six years separated the girls in age, the scans showed that their abnormal brains were identical – with one exception. "See here," she pointed as she continued to speak. This time we could make out what she was pointing to. Little white patches were visible on Cheryl's scan; whereas Joy's had none. The doctor went on to say that she couldn't be absolutely sure of the cause of these strange patches, but they did indicate little areas of damage to the brain tissue. "Perhaps her seizures have caused the damage," she theorized, "or it may be an indication of straightforward degeneration of the brain." We didn't like the sound of either, but were left with the impression that Northern Ireland's only paediatric neurologist thought that Cheryl's condition was deteriorating. In fact it was her impression that Cheryl wouldn't have "too many birthdays left". But I held on to the fact that no-one really knew how much time Cheryl had left – except the One who made her. And so I put on my stoical face and we took both girls home, where we could get on with the business of being a family. However the thought crossed my mind that maybe it was about time we starting talking to Paul about Heaven, and what that would mean for Cheryl. (I suppose denial caused me not to include Joy in the equation at that time!)

"Will Cheryl be able to eat potato crisps when she goes to Heaven?" seemed like a perfectly logical question for a five year old to ask! Paul often lamented over the fact that Cheryl was unable to enjoy such delights, and if Heaven meant Cheryl could eat all the goodies that she missed here, then maybe Heaven would be okay. While wanting to get across the reality of Heaven as an actual place, where pain and suffering would not be present, it was rather difficult to get the theology simple enough for a youngster to understand. We wanted Paul to know that one day his sister would get a 'new' body, and one that would work perfectly. So with the help of his children's bible, and other books especially written for children, we brought up the subject of dying every now and then over the next few years. Death is still one of the great taboos for discussing with our children; yet I have found that if approached properly, preparation can be a great help to a child when someone they love dies. Many of their questions will have already been answered to some extent, and that in itself helps to reduce the element of fear.

Fear of the unknown can conjure up all kinds of imaginings. As his parents, Philip and I wanted Paul to know about death in a way that was neither morbid nor would make him afraid. Even more, we wanted him to know about Heaven – after all, it must surely be the greatest promise ever given by God to those who are His children! While not wanting to dwell unreasonably on the topic, we found that it was Paul who inquired at the most unusual of times about what was going to happen to Cheryl.

One day, my hands were full with pushing our specially adapted twin buggy, and Paul was riding circles around us on his bicycle, on the way to the local shops. The girls nearly landed under his wheels when he stopped abruptly right across our path! "Paul!" I shouted in rebuke, while pulling the large buggy to a stop. But before I had a chance to continue he looked at me intently and said: "Mummy, will Cheryl be able to ride a bike when she comes back from Heaven?" The question floored me, and the public situation was not a suitable place for an answer that might upset him. "Let's keep that question for Daddy when we get home," I quickly replied, explaining that he needed to concentrate when he was cycling, or he would cause an accident! With his attention diverted for a while, I groaned inside: "He must think that Heaven is a bit like going on holiday – when you've had your fun, you come back home again." Later we gently told him that when you go to Heaven it's for good – you don't come back, but your family can come to you when they die. His face became contorted in thought, and then he announced: "Don't think I like that – I want Cheryl to come back when she gets her new body and then she can play with me!"

It was just as matter-of-fact as that. He wasn't upset; he had just decided for now that he would rather she came back and that was that! Reasoning would have served no purpose at the time, and so we let that part of his childish rationale remain – it was enough for now.

***

Joy was very like Cheryl in her disabilities, but that was all. Cheryl had a quiet, gentle nature. She was a patient child, and by the time she was eight years old her hair was still blonde and wavy, setting off beautiful blue eyes. Joy, on the other hand, at two years old was wriggly, giggly and full of personality. She responded to tickling, and could (sometimes!) be calmed by music – much to her brother's delight! Her hair was a mousey dirty fair colour, like her brother's, and as straight as a poker!

As Cheryl became weaker her days were becoming quieter, while, on the other hand, Joy's days were filling up with Nursery School, appointments and therapists! Joy only crossed town to Segal House for two terms, as a new nursery class had opened at the school where Cheryl was a pupil. It was strange; yet comforting to see them head off in the morning together. And for the first time in two years I had a few hours each day to myself – it was wonderful!

By this stage Cheryl was spending most of her days asleep – nature's way of conserving her limited energy for the important tasks. Feeding continued to take hours every day, as her swallowing problems increased, along with the recurring stomach symptoms. There was no suggestion of further surgery, and so a variety of medicines was tried to alleviate the discomfort. Unfortunately some medications can interact badly with others, and on one occasion Cheryl was rendered unconscious by that very problem! It was a major learning curve for all the doctors concerned, and resulted in the doctor in overall charge of her care insisting that she be made aware of *any* change in Cheryl's medication. We had no intention of making it into a big issue as there was no doubt that our daughter was receiving the best care possible from a group of wonderful paediatricians. Added to which, once the alterations in the regime were made we got back a slightly more awake Cheryl!

Caring for Cheryl at home as much as possible was very important to me, and because of my nursing skills, I was able to achieve this most of the time. The school physio was also amazing, and when Cheryl had one of her frequent chest infections, she came to treat her at home. When Cheryl was in hospital it caused the added pressure of being away from Joy, and rearranging Paul's schedule too. Thankfully, because Philip worked from home, he and my parents managed, while I spent my days with Cheryl (and sometimes the nights too, if necessary).

And so we entered what I called the 'Roller Coaster' season of our lives with Cheryl. It's undoubtedly one of the hardest parts of caring for a life limited child. You are brought to the edge of your physical and emotional strength so many times, it becomes exhausting! For weeks you could be making a slow ascent, when everything seems to be improving, and you dare to get excited that maybe the doctor was wrong – maybe she will see her next birthday after all. Then suddenly you plummet down to the depths of despair, feeling that you will never recover from being this far down. And then you turn a corner, levelling out once more, and watch the child you love start to climb again. All the while knowing that another drop is just ahead – except that you don't know where or when!

Thankfully, Cheryl didn't seem to be in too much pain. Her big problem was that her deformed rib cage made it so easy for chest infections to settle, while also making chest physiotherapy less effective. We had battled through predictions of gloom for three birthdays and three Christmas seasons. She looked pathetically thin and slept for most of the time, yet seemed to rally after every illness. And we loved her so much more than words could ever convey.

Time and again when I lifted her in my arms I would talk to her about Heaven, just as I had with little Baby Barbara ten years previously. Because we are spiritual beings, I believe that God's Holy Spirit can reach into the places we know so little about. And so I would pray that He would give Cheryl His peace – as only He could. When things were difficult, and she struggled for breath, I would sing to her of the promise that God had given to me:"It will be worth it all...when we see Jesus." Later many people remarked on how they felt that Cheryl had such a peace about her – it was almost like an aura. And I knew that God had answered my prayer.

*****

I wakened with a start, and looked at the clock. It was nearly eight o'clock – we had overslept! This was unheard of, as we rarely got more than three hours continuous sleep, and the girls (especially Joy) were always awake by six o'clock in the morning. Philip jumped out of bed to waken Paul for school, while I rushed into the girls' room. Joy was awake and had wriggled under her duvet. If she had been able to speak I'm sure she would have cried:"Quickly Mummy, rescue me! I'm roasting under here!" A big smile crossed her face as I lifted her out of the bed, and handed her to her bedraggled daddy as he came into the room. "Well, who's been a good girl, then," he said, "letting Mummy and Daddy have a lie in?" She continued to charm us as I looked at Cheryl's sleeping form in the bed opposite to Joy's. "Come on, Sleepyhead," I said to Cheryl, "you'll never be ready in time for the bus this morning." As I bent over to pull back the duvet cover, I realized something was wrong. Her breathing was laboured, and her forehead was very hot as I planted my 'good morning' kiss on it. "Oh no, Cheryl," I groaned. "You're not going to come down with this flu – are you, Sweetheart?" (In December 1989, the news was full of reports of the flu epidemic that was sweeping the country.) She didn't even twitch as I lifted her out of the bed, and she just hung limp in my arms as I carried her downstairs.

Philip had already started giving Joy her Readybrek when I entered the living room. His look darkened as he watched me prop Cheryl up on the settee. "What's wrong, Catherine?" he asked anxiously. "I think she might have this flu," I replied. "She just won't waken up." I always tried to play down a crisis with Philip and Paul, until we were sure that one really existed. So I encouraged Philip to continue getting Joy ready for school, while geeing Paul up at the same time. After quickly sponging Cheryl down, and giving her some rectal medication, to help bring her temperature down, I made the decision to ring the doctor. Miraculously, I got through at the first attempt, and as soon as I reported that Cheryl could not be roused, one of the GPs came immediately. As the health centre was only a short distance away, she arrived within minutes.

"There's not much air moving in her lungs, Catherine," the doctor said after sounding her chest. "I think we need to get her into hospital." Perhaps it was denial of the seriousness of her condition, or genuinely because I thought she would be better away from hospital during a flu epidemic, that I persuaded the doctor to let her stay until I could get in touch with the school physio. I felt sure that if her temperature came down, and she had some chest physiotherapy, that she would waken up and be able to take the antibiotics that the doctor had left for her. The doctor was not convinced, but gave me a little leeway. "You have one hour," she said as she left. "If Cheryl is no better by then, she has to be admitted."

It was still before nine o'clock and, as Philip was leaving to take Paul to school, I was trying the physio's phone number at school. About seven minutes later she was in our living room with her hands on Cheryl's chest. "Please Catherine," she pleaded, "take her to hospital? She is very sick!" Within a few minutes, the doctor was phoned once again, and we were on our way to the ward, transported in the physio's car. Philip remained behind to see Joy on to the school bus, with the promise that he would follow on behind. And still Cheryl didn't wake up!

I don't know what the doctor had said to the ward staff, but they were ready and waiting for us when we arrived. I was so glad that we didn't have to sit and wait in A&E, because although I appeared calm on the exterior, I was beginning to see just how sick Cheryl really was. My heart was racing, but as I discovered, not racing nearly as fast as Cheryl's!

The ward doctor quickly examined our little girl, who was now fighting for her life. An intravenous line was in place in no time, and the first dose of antibiotics followed soon after. Monitors were put in place, oxygen administered and the portable x-ray machine was trundled in and out again before Philip arrived. By the time he did, Cheryl looked really ill. "If only I'd kept her at home," I thought. "She always looks worse when they attach all that equipment," I tried to convince myself. My deep longing to try to protect my darling child from this moment showed itself in my denying that she was so sick. I tried all the comforting words that I knew on Philip, trying to convince him that everything was going to be okay. "She's come through it before, she'll do it again," I said reassuringly. Philip sat quietly as I rattled on. He was finding the hospitalizations harder and harder to bear, as with each one Cheryl grew weaker. And now lying in the bed she looked so weary, and I was afraid that she was tired of fighting.

The doctor appeared with an x-ray in his hand. He pulled up a chair, and with a sigh he started to speak: "I'm afraid things don't look too good. Cheryl has patches of pneumonia in both lungs." We made no reply, waiting for the 'but' that would assure us that it was only a matter of time before things improved. The 'but' didn't come. Instead he told us that the consultant had been informed of Cheryl's admission, and that she would come and speak to us after her clinic. After he left, someone brought us a cup of tea. (I'm always suspicious of 'cups of tea' given without being requested – they smack of bad news, and are usually ordered by someone who knows more about what's going on than you do!) At least drinking it gave us something to do, as we each escaped into our own thoughts. Soon Philip was on his way home to let the family know what was going on, and to make contact with the many prayer groups who had prayed for Cheryl in the past.

Once alone, I found a little space in the oxygen tent to slip my hand through. As I held Cheryl's tiny hand the tears welled up, and silently journeyed down my cheeks. She had been here so many times before and had always proved the doctors wrong by getting better. It was less than three weeks to Christmas – she couldn't die now! My heart felt like a stone in my chest, as I closed my eyes and prayed for the first time since wakening that morning. "Don't let her die, God, please!" was all I could say.

By lunchtime, the consultant had been to see Cheryl. "I don't know if she'll see Christmas," was all I remember her saying. "But you said that *last* year," I reminded her, "and she did." The consultant ordered the oxygen tent taken down and replaced with a more traditional mask. It was good to be able to stroke Cheryl's face again. I longed to hold her, but was discouraged from doing so, as the staff thought it would restrict her breathing. Soon Philip returned, and during the day family members came back and forward, helping to fill the long day as we sat and waited. But still Cheryl didn't wake up.

As the week was passing, I made the odd foray home for a shower and to visit the children, while Philip stayed with Cheryl. Occasionally I brought Paul back with me when Philip and I changed shifts. We had discovered on a previous occasion that Paul fretted far more if he didn't get to see Cheryl, than he did when we tried to protect him by keeping him away. His visits usually consisted of a "Hello" to his sister, and then a trip to the ward play area, which was 'cool'! Although it was a very difficult week, we experienced what I called the 'cotton wool treatment'. We were so aware of other people praying for us, and for Cheryl, that we felt 'wrapped up' in the love and consideration of others. Sometimes I felt that Philip had the harder job, as he had to field numerous phone calls when he returned from the hospital late at night.

And still Cheryl did not wake up! When the consultant visited on Friday, there was still no change – except for the fact that now she too had the flu, as did poor little Joy, who had been moved to Granny's for extra care!

***

Saturday morning came with a sense of excitement in the ward. Many of the children were out of their beds very early, and giggles were coming from the play area. I walked up the ward to see what was going on. "We just can't settle them down," the nurse explained as I approached, "so we've decided to let them start by making paper decorations." Strips of coloured sticky paper filled the table, as happy little hands excitedly made them into links for the growing paper chain. "The Christmas decorations go up today," she continued, in a voice raised above the happy chatter. I had almost forgotten about Christmas as I had spent all week in a four-bedded ward!

When I returned to Cheryl's bedside, and was about to tell her about all the activity in the play area, I noticed something that made me gasp! Cheryl's eyes were open – she was awake! I turned on my heels and ran for the nurse. Neither of us could believe it. Cheryl moved her head, and her arms wriggled by her side. I thought I was going to explode! She'd done it – she'd done it again! Already, in my mind, I was planning the great escape! A couple of days and she would be eating again, and then we'd get her home. Home for Christmas!!

I rushed out to the phone to tell Philip the great news. Soon the word would get around that Cheryl was getting better! She'd really done it!

After a little while I was able to wash and dress her, and although she had a sleep afterward; it was a normal sleep. And I wasn't the only one who was excited. The children on the ward all seemed to know that the little girl who had been asleep all week had woken up – and they were excited too. In fact, shortly after nine o'clock, a small group of children were allowed to come into the unit where Cheryl, and other very sick children, were being nursed. They had decorations in their hands! Tinsel was tied to Cheryl's cot, and a big picture of Santa was stuck to the wall close by. "That's for Cheryl to see, now that she's awake," the little boy said proudly. "I'm sure she'll love it," I replied, not wanting to spoil his fun by telling him that Cheryl couldn't see!

I waited impatiently for the first visitors to arrive – I just wanted someone to share in my excitement. I was able to hold Cheryl for the first time all week, and she seemed to manage it very well. Her bony little frame felt wonderful in my arms, and when Granny sang to her later that afternoon she even let out a gentle: "Ahh." Smiles replaced frowns, and praise replaced prayer. Everyone who saw her that day was rejoicing!

And so, later that evening Philip suggested that I go home for a sleep in my own bed, while he stayed on in the ward with Cheryl. "I'll come home later if she's settled, and you can come back in if you want. Go on," he coaxed, "Paul would be so glad to see you for a wee while." The thought was enticing, and so I went home, secure in the thought that I would see Cheryl later.

Paul was in lively mood when I picked him up from Granny's to take him home. Joy would stay there so that I could get a good rest, and I was looking forward to having all of my family together again soon. The two of us sat and talked over his week, and he told me all about school, and his friends, and how glad he was that Cheryl was getting better. At eight years old, he loved to please, and was still very affectionate with his kisses and hugs. After talking for a while he jumped down off the sofa, and disappeared. I had no idea what he was doing, but when he reappeared I was bowled over by his thoughtfulness. He approached me with a tea towel neatly over one arm, like a waiter, and handed me a handwritten menu as he spoke. "Madam, can I get you something to drink?" he said putting on a posh accent. On the menu were written the words: TEA OR ORANGE JUICE

TOAST OR BISCUIT

"What's all this?" I said to him proudly. "I know you're tired Mummy, and I just want to give you a treat," he replied, and then reverted to his actor's voice. "So Madam, what would you like?" I didn't fancy explaining a scalding to a casualty doctor, so I choose the orange juice and biscuit, which came served on a lovely tray complete with napkin! The thought, however, was much more appreciated than the food!

Once Paul was safely tucked into bed, I propped myself against the pillows and lifted my book of daily readings that I hadn't touched all week, and contentedly started to read. I had barely finished the first paragraph when the words I was reading caused me to gasp!

"Be strong, my soul!
Thy loved ones go
Within the veil, God's thine, e'en so;
Be strong.

Be strong, my soul!
Death looms in view.
Lo, here thy God! He'll bear thee through;
Be strong."   (Anon)

I closed the book and threw it down. "No! It can't be true!" I exclaimed. "Cheryl is getting better. That word isn't for me. It can't be!" The ringing of the phone interrupted the frightening thought that I had just read. It was my friend and we spent the next few minutes talking about how Cheryl had made a fool of the doctors once again. Soon, sleep overtook me.

I was exhausted, yet years of 'listening' while sleeping, incase the girls wakened, meant that I woke up in response to the slightest sound. Philip was home, and I sat up as I heard his footsteps on the stairs. He looked tired, as he related how the evening had gone. We decided to set the alarm clock for 2am, in order that I could go back to the ward. Philip was not as happy with Cheryl's condition as he had been earlier, but he felt that I should get a bit more sleep before returning. The staff nurse in charge was one we particularly respected, and she had promised to phone us if there was any deterioration before then. And so I settled down to sleep again for another few hours, while Philip went downstairs to get a cup of tea.

Warm breath on my face started to waken me. In the distance I could hear my name being called ever so gently through my sleep: "Catherine, Catherine." In my semi-wakened state I realized it was Philip's voice, and I suddenly opened my eyes to see him kneeling beside the bed! I knew what he was going to tell me as soon as I saw his tear-stained face. A look of deep pain stared back at me: "She's gone!" he wept! "Our little girl is gone!"

'Be strong, my soul!' author unknown.
Source, Streams in the Desert Vol. 1 by Mrs Charles E Cowan

Seven

The Final Farewell

HOW Paul stayed asleep through the noise of that night, I will never know. My mind was in a whirl, with grief and questions battling for prime position. "She couldn't be dead!" I yelled at my upset husband. "They would never tell you that over the phone – you're wrong!" His attempts at comfort were met with sheer distress, as my world fell apart around me. "How could we have left her to die alone?!" I wept. "Why did the nurse not phone us in time? We should have been with her!" My voice lost its strength as I stopped fighting the man I loved so much, and I fell into his arms: "We have to go to her – now – quickly!"

A sickening, hollow, emptiness replaced the tears as I sat in the front seat of the car, listening to my mother trying to stifle her sobs as she sat behind me. My poor dad was staying with Joy, and a neighbour waited for my friend to arrive, to be in the house in case Paul woke up. On the way to the hospital we stopped with Philip's parents to give them the awful news that their first grandchild was dead – they followed on soon after.

We travelled in silence for the rest of the short journey. Ironically, there was no problem parking close to the entrance tonight, and all was quiet as we walked down the seemingly endless corridor to the ward. Irrational feelings of hatred rose to the surface as I blamed 'this place' for taking my daughter. Those foolish thoughts disappeared as we entered the ward, where I knew that Cheryl had been lovingly cared for – I just resented having to need it so much over these past ten years!

All was quiet in the semi-darkness. No babies were crying – no children coughing. The silence assumed a respectful reverence for the child that had just been lost. The space where her bed had been was now empty – the smiling face of the big Santa now totally out of place. A door opened, and out of a side-ward appeared the nurse-in-charge. She hurried toward me with her arms open wide, and whispered: "I'm so sorry," as she held me. Directing us through a door, we entered the nicely lit side-ward. I was speechless as she explained what had happened, and also her concern that the night-sister had made the decision to tell Philip over the phone that Cheryl had died at 12.30am.

But she didn't look dead to me – she was lying propped up on her V-shaped pillow, just like she did every night. And she was *so* beautiful. Her blonde wavy hair was sitting perfectly, and her lovely clear skin just seemed to glow. Her beautiful hands rested on the pink bed cover, displaying neatly trimmed nails – a tribute to the loving preparations the nurse had made when getting Cheryl ready for our arrival. There was no distress on her face, no fear, and no sign of the week-long struggle she had endured. The nurse had dressed her in a lovely pink and blue cotton dress along with white knee-length lacy socks. What the nurse didn't know was that it was her last birthday dress – bought for her tenth birthday, just four months earlier!

The nurse was still speaking as I was taking in the scene, and, in a surreal way, I heard her relate how she went to change Cheryl's position after midnight. "I slipped my arms under her, and turned her over," she was explaining. "When she landed on her other side she was gone ... my arms were still under her ... she was alive on one side – and not on the other. It really was that quick! She didn't deteriorate – honestly, I would have called you if there had been any sign of change!" She struggled to find the words that she needed to explain herself: "It was as if ... " "She was lifted," my mother interrupted. "That's exactly what I was trying to say!" the nurse exclaimed.

"She was lifted by God, Love," my mum said, trying to be reassuring, as she slipped her arm around my waist. "Why didn't God allow me to be with her when He came to take her?" I answered, feeling cheated. "Tonight was the first night I had gone home! She was awake earlier – she was getting better!" I protested. The tender response from my husband caused a momentary silence to fall in the room. "Cheryl needed you to live, Catherine - she didn't need you to die," he said, trying to help me deal with the guilt and betrayal that was overwhelming me.

Soon Cheryl was in my arms, and I was so glad of the opportunity we had all had earlier that day to hold her. My tears splashing on her face couldn't awaken her, and my cuddles couldn't cause her bony little body any further pain. She looked at peace, and I knew, as I held her, that she wasn't here any more. She was now enjoying the Heaven that I had told her about so many times; now experiencing the new body that had caused so much questioning from Paul. She wouldn't be home for Christmas and yet this would be the first Christmas she would *really* enjoy. The tinsel that the children had attached earlier was still glittering on her cot, almost mocking us!

The ward staff were wonderful, as they allowed us so much time with Cheryl. Other family members were allowed to come and go – to give their beloved grandchild or niece one last cuddle. As I watched my dear dad hold his darling Cheryl, I understood what the term 'broken hearted' really meant. And the words that I had rejected earlier that night echoed in my mind: "Be strong, my soul! Lo, here thy God! *He'll bear thee through*; be strong!" And the unspoken prayer of my heart didn't have far to travel, because God was already in the room: "Help me to be strong Lord!"

Around 3.30am, on the 10th of December, 1989, I closed the door of the hospital side-ward – never to hold my beautiful, brave daughter again. She had been 'lifted' into the arms of someone else who loved her, the One who said many years ago: "Let the little children come to me . . . for of such is the kingdom of Heaven." (Matt 19:14) And so we headed home to await the dawn, and to tell Paul that his 'big' sister had died.

Philip had persuaded me to slip into bed again while we waited for Paul to waken. When Paul had gone to bed the night before, his daddy was still at the hospital. Now Philip was sitting, fully dressed, on the side of the bed, when Paul's little shape walked past our open door to the bathroom. It was 6am – he was always an early- bird. As he came back out he looked into our room, and saw his daddy by the dim light of our bedside lamp. Taking stock of the situation quickly, he asked; "Are you only just home, Daddy? Why have you still got your clothes on?" Philip beckoned him in: "Jump in beside Mummy," he said, trying to maintain his composure as he helped Paul into our bed.

Bright child that he was, he guessed something was going on, and said: "What's wrong, Daddy?" as he pulled the duvet around him against the cold. Philip's voice seemed remarkably strong as the words came: "Cheryl died during the night, Paul. She was just too sick, Son, and so God took her to Heaven, where she won't be sick any more." Paul's little hand went to his face as he smothered a gasp, and in that instant he pushed me away. His whole body stiffened and he turned his back on us, as if we had betrayed him. I tried to dam back the tears that had formed as I heard Philip use the word 'died' to Paul.

We gave him a little space, as he tried to process the kind of news no eight year old should have to hear. I wanted to speak – to tell him that it wasn't true. I wanted to protect him from the pain that was starting to invade his young life. But there was nothing I could do – no way could I avoid the truth that two weeks before Christmas, we had lost our daughter, and he had lost his sister! And in that moment he didn't even want us to touch him.

"It's okay to be sad, Paul. It's okay to cry," encouraged Philip. Paul's silence was broken as he quickly turned to face us. His expression was one of anger and betrayal: "You didn't tell me she was going to die!" he said, accusingly. As I reached towards him I was shocked by his statement. "But . . ." I stammered. "We told you lots of times that Cheryl would die one day, and go to Heaven." "But, you didn't tell me she was going to die *last* night!" He threw himself into my arms, and the floodgates broke for us all. "We didn't know she was going to die last night, Sweetheart!" was all I could say. For a while the three of us lay together wrapped in grief, yet wrapped in love for each other. I wanted to shut the door of that room and never have to leave, but there were other people who loved Cheryl, and as the world was waking up, we needed to tell them the news.

***

The next few days were a mixture of intense sadness and tangible peace. It has always amazed me how emotions that are poles apart can co-exist in the same person. Just as Ireland can experience four seasons in one day; so I experienced anger, sadness, peace and even happiness during the days leading up to the funeral. As people, literally from all over the world, prayed for us we knew the sustaining power of God. In fact, often I was the one who comforted folk as they came to our home to offer their sympathy!

Cards, flowers, phone calls, and visitors poured into our home with frequent regularity. We talked to people from places as far apart as Belfast and Bolivia! Letters written by doctors, nurses and therapists, who had all played a big part in Cheryl surviving as long as she did, brought us great comfort and pride. Most of them referred to her bravery as she endured difficult procedures, and said how proud they were to have cared for her. One surgeon even apologized that he had been unable to do more to relieve her suffering.

Our home seemed to be constantly full of people, which helped us get through the long days before the funeral. While some people prefer 'house private', I feel that we would have missed so much of the comfort and support we received from having our home open to visitors. My kitchen was organized in my absence by a whole team of 'ministering angels' led by both of our own two loving sisters, and other friends. People were fed at all times of the day and I was happy to do as I was told – and to stay out of the kitchen!

We were glad, on a few occasions, to be able to escape and go to see Joy, who was still at my parents' home recovering from flu. Holding her brought relief to my empty arms. She was totally unaware of all that was going on, and as she was so well looked after by my parents, I don't think she even missed me! My mum had told this wee mite that Cheryl had gone on to

Heaven before her, and Joy responded as she usually did when someone held her and talked to her – she smiled! Joy wouldn't grieve as we would – and for that I was thankful.

In Ireland, many families still bring their loved one's remains home until the funeral. It is both traumatic and enormously comforting. To have Cheryl rest in her small white coffin on top of her own bed, in her own room, was just as it should be, as far as we were concerned. Many of our friends and family were able to have precious time alone with her during those few days. There was just one problem . . . Paul would have brought the whole neighbourhood in to see Cheryl, if we had let him!

Paul had decided he wanted to go to school until the funeral, and so we agreed that a bit of normality might be good for him. Poor Philip had all the hard jobs to do. So when Paul insisted on going to school, Philip went with him and spoke to his teacher privately to let her know what had happened. We also wanted to ensure that if Paul became fretful she would contact us. However, if we had known beforehand that the staff at the school would have ignored Cheryl's death, I think we would have kept him home. It's sad to think that professionals trained in working with children, avoided speaking to a child about a sibling's death. Any excuse rings hollow – especially the one that says "We didn't want to make him sad." He was already sad! Instead, the only person to sympathize with our son at school that day was his little classmate, who gave him a neck hug and said: "Hey, Paul, I'm sorry your sister died."

During the time that Paul was at school, Cheryl's remains arrived home. Later he burst in through the front door at the speed of light, and I had to chase upstairs after him to stop him from running into her room! He impatiently listened while changing out of his school uniform, as I tried to prepare him for what he would see. "Just let's go, Mum!" he said, unwilling to wait any longer. I was nervous, but Paul was, dare I say it – excited. He had been disappointed when he heard other family members talk about seeing Cheryl the night she died, when he hadn't been given the same opportunity. So now it was his turn, and he wanted to see his sister!

He quietened the moment we entered her room. "She looks like she's sleeping, mummy," he commented, glancing at me sideways. Then he pulled his hand away quickly as he touched her: "She's freezing!" he shouted. I explained to him that one of the ways we know that the real Cheryl doesn't live in her body anymore is that it's very cold. He never touched her again. My talk to him about the new body she now had in Heaven was obviously not as interesting as the coffin – he was really taken with it, and talked a lot about it!

Soon he was off to play with his friends at the house next door. Ten minutes later he was back, asking if his friends could see Cheryl and her nice coffin too!! (While I believe that what children imagine about death is often worse than the reality, and that it is therefore good to include them in what is going on – a line does need to be drawn!) After discussing the issue of why some people could see Cheryl and perhaps others shouldn't, Paul was told that only those children who knew her well would be allowed to see her – and only with their parents present! As you can imagine, that whittled it down to a few very close friends, whose children said they would like to say good-bye to Cheryl.

The night before the funeral, Paul went in to see Cheryl before he went to bed. It was obvious that he was troubled about something, and so I sat him on my knee to give him the chance to get it off his chest. His response shouldn't have surprised me, as children often think about things that wouldn't cross our minds: "Will you put her coffin in a plastic bag tomorrow, mummy?" he said, looking rather worried. "It's such a lovely, white coffin, and it will get very dirty if the grave men put muck on it!" There I was, concerned over what deep, searching question this eight year old was going to ask, and all he wanted to know was how we would keep the coffin clean!

***

I woke very early in the morning, and tiptoed into the next room, not wanting to disturb Philip and Paul earlier than necessary on this most dreaded of days. Today we would say our final farewell to our firstborn – our beautiful, gentle Cheryl. And as I looked at her I didn't know how I would be able to let her leave this house – let alone, leave our lives. I spent the next little while talking to her – even though I knew she couldn't hear me. I wanted her to know, once more, how sorry I was that I hadn't been with her when she died. I wanted her to know how much I loved her, and how I would always love her. And I wanted her to know that it would be just a little while before I would be with her again – only then she would be able to talk back to me! In the cool of that room, the emptiness of my heart was filled with a strange sense that she already knew these things.

My mother/daughter time was finally brought to an end as I felt a hand on my shoulder. It was Philip. "Did I waken you?" I asked. "No," was his simple reply. "Soon the house will be full," I said. "Why don't you have a little time on your own with her, while I go and get ready?" "Okay," was all he said as I let him sit on the warm chair. We had been married for twelve years, and didn't always need a lot of words to communicate what was on our hearts. As I left the room, I could picture his face on the day she was born – that look of pride and delight! "Please God, help him today?" I pleaded.

The morning passed quickly before the family arrived for the short service at home, which was to precede the main funeral service at the church. As the undertaker arrived I had this overwhelming urge to send him away. "Perhaps he could come another day," I panicked, "it's too soon to let her go!" He was my friend's father, and that brought me some comfort, as I didn't want just anyone to handle her. I know that in the past he had prayed for her, and so when he hugged me that day and said: "Don't worry, Catherine, I'll look after her" – I knew he would.

As I looked around the room, I could see that all those who loved both us, and Cheryl, were there. The arrival of my brother from Germany the previous day had completed the family circle. God had been so good to give both Philip and me such strong, supportive families. Today, of all days, we needed them.

"Be strong, my soul." I whispered. And God replied: "I'll bear thee through!" And He kept His promise once more, as I felt myself strangely enabled during the service, and especially as Cheryl left our home for the last time.

The large church we attended was well filled when we arrived, even though many apologies had been received because people were still affected by the flu epidemic. As I looked around the congregation I was humbled to see so many people gathered to pay tribute to a little girl, whom some people might have regarded as a burden to society. Yet Cheryl had touched the lives of many in her ten short years. She had taught us all how to display patience in adversity, to live without grumbling, and even how to see beyond ourselves to the needs of others. Her life was certainly no waste, but rather one that I believe 'glorified God,' and now she is 'enjoying Him forever' (as the Presbyterian catechism would put it).

Standing in church before a small white coffin, with a teddy bear wreath placed on top, seemed so unnatural. Children aren't supposed to die before their parents – it's not how it should happen. And as I realized that that white coffin held my *own* child, I felt at that moment it held my heart too.

Good friends bravely took part in the service, and God gave them amazing grace as they did so – especially our friend (host of the Cloughey circus!) who delivered a wonderful tribute to Cheryl. My heart swelled within me as I heard him speak of all the ways in which her life had blessed and challenged others. Every now and then Paul would glance up at me, or tap my arm and give a little reassuring smile, agreeing with all that was being said. The minister, who had dedicated Cheryl ten years before, returned to speak at her funeral. He chose a phrase from Jeremiah 15:9 as his text: "Her sun has gone down, while it was yet day." Within that powerful sermon was the most comforting of thoughts: "The sun sets on one horizon that it might rise in another!" What a beautiful description of death – setting in one horizon, while simultaneously rising in another. And I remembered what the nurse had said a few short days before – "on one side she was alive, and on the other side –'she had been lifted!' " Cheryl had a seamless passing indeed.

The service was over, and our family turned to follow Cheryl's coffin as it exited the church. Then an amazing thing happened!

My gaze was fixed on the coffin as it made its way down the aisle. An overwhelming feeling of pride came over me as I thought of Cheryl, and God gave me, what I can only describe as a beautiful picture of what was happening to her. I'm not into 'visions', or the like, but I believe this picture was God, in His mercy, allowing me to know that all was well with Cheryl.

I saw Cheryl running up a long path towards Jesus, who had His arms opened wide. He was bending down towards her, and as He scooped her up, and swung her around, I heard Him say clearly: "Well done, Pet. You've been such a good girl!" It came in a flash and was gone just as quickly – but in that instant I knew that God had welcomed her home . . . and that He was pleased with her! She had received the glorious welcome she deserved.

I didn't go to the cemetery, where the sleet of that cold December day lashed the mourners relentlessly, and where God answered my prayers for Philip, and gave him help.

***

Children grieve very differently from the way adults do, and depending on their age and circumstances, they can even grieve differently from one child to another. The well documented stages of grief – shock, denial, anger, sadness and acceptance – are also experienced by children. It is therefore very important to watch for changes in behaviour that may appear to have nothing to do with the child's loss, but which may in fact have everything to do with it. Regression to behaviour associated with a younger age, is the most common form of non-verbal communication children can use when seeking attention for their loss. Often children cannot explain their behaviour – they genuinely have no idea what's wrong with them. Also there is no accepted length of time for each of the stages of grief, or what order they come in – apart from acceptance, which is last . . . unless the other stages are revisited!

One of the best ways to help our children grieve is in preparation. Not merely in preparing them for a death – because not all deaths are expected. Some are very sudden. The best form of preparation is in having a good relationship with our children. They will not find it easy to talk over the sadness in their hearts, if they have not previously been used to talking to us about everyday issues.

It's true that not all children are talkers. But all children can be taught to engage in conversation by our persistence! We need to learn to use open-ended questions from the time they are very young. Getting them used to sharing things will form the good habit of openness within a family. And it will pay dividends, because there will come a day when our children will need to talk – and we want it to be us they talk to.

We were very fortunate – Paul was always a talker! He could speak in sentences before he was brave enough to walk! And he knew from his first class that his mummy would never be satisfied with "Okay" as the answer to the question: "How did school go today?" So we talked to him about everything that was appropriate, while he found it easier just to tell us everything! That way he knew we cared about every area of his life, and then as he grew older it was less difficult for him to open up, when he needed to.

Well, that was the theory – and you know what they say about theories – they don't always work, as I found out! Shortly after Cheryl died I was feeling very sorry that Paul had no 'normal' siblings, and I came off with one of those throw-away comments. Not really expecting an answer from my eight year old son I said: "I'm sure it hasn't always been easy for you, Son, having two handicapped sisters?" Without changing his position, he replied: "It's just hard when other boys call you names, and say 'You're a plastic spastic like your sisters!'" I nearly fell off my chair! "Who said that?" I demanded to know. "Why didn't you tell me about this?" I went on to say in my shock, hardly giving Paul time to reply.

"They're just not nice boys, Mummy, and anyway, my sisters aren't plastic spastics! What do they know?" He appeared unperturbed, yet I knew it must have hurt him at the time, or he wouldn't have brought it up even now. For him it was over, but for me it was yet another hurt he had endured because of his sisters.

In general, we were able to talk with Paul about most things, but usually only when he was ready. It would be Christmas in less than two weeks, and for now that was what occupied most of his thinking. Because I am a fairly organized person, some of the Christmas gift shopping had already been done before Cheryl had gone into hospital. The rest was left undone, apart from one day when Philip took me out of our area to escape the house for a little while. We wandered around a large shop, amazed to see the rest of the world carrying on with their business as if nothing had happened. I wanted to yell at the shoppers: "Don't you realize that our little girl is dead!" It was unreal to me, that 'normal things' could be going on while we were in a state of deep sadness.

I love Christmas. I always have, and always will. Not merely because of decorations, gifts, and family visits. I love Christmas because it spells *hope* – it reminds me that God poured hope into a world that had no hope, spiritually speaking. Every one of us is hopeless because of our sin - separated from a holy God, not only for now but also for eternity. Without God, the meaning of life evades us, and we are denied a personal relationship with the only One who can fill up the empty places with His peace and purpose. St. Augustine said: "Thou hast made us for Thyself, and our hearts are restless, 'til they find their rest in Thee." However, on that first Christmas, God set about putting the hope back, by sending His Son Jesus into this world to be our Saviour – once more making it possible for us to have a relationship with our Creator through repentance and faith. Hope for the hopeless was restored – that's why I love Christmas!

Now, on this saddest of all Christmases, I was still preparing to celebrate – not merely because I had other children, but because Christmas spelt *hope* to me in bigger letters than ever. Without the Saviour, my loss would be totally pointless! He, it was, who gave me not only the hope, but the assurance that He makes no mistakes … that He understands my pain, and is with me in it … that He welcomed Cheryl into Heaven … and that one day I will be with her again. How could I not celebrate the season of the year that reminds us of the kind of hope that only God can give?!

Undoubtedly Christmas would be different from now on, but whereas happiness depends on happenings, joy does not. And so Christmas came - with much sadness, and many tears, yet with joy in the experience of God's love surrounding me.

There were even some smiles as we watched Paul enjoy his somewhat smaller than usual pile of presents. And Philip presented me with a beautiful photograph album of Cheryl, (which he had compiled on late nights after I had gone to bed) – probably the most precious Christmas present I have ever been given! We also used the album as a conversation starter with Paul, whenever we would look over it together. He loved looking at the pictures, and we did spend some time laughing too, especially at the captions Philip had written under them.

Different pictures would bring out differing memories. When looking at one of Cheryl and Joy lying at either end of the settee, like a pair of bookends, Paul suddenly said: "Mum, do you remember the night Cheryl smiled?" And we discussed together the delight we both had at witnessing her last smile just months before she died. Since being very ill with measles around the age of eight, Cheryl had rarely, if ever smiled (this was attributed to further brain damage caused by the measles). One night the girls were both lying in their pyjamas at either end of the settee (just like in the picture), when Joy took a fit of the giggles! Paul loved to hear Joy laugh, and he was keeping the laughter going by tickling her knees. I was about to break up the teasing when he suddenly announced: "Look mummy, Cheryl is smiling – she's really smiling!" True enough, Cheryl was actually responding to the raucous giggling and laughter in the room. For at least a minute the big, broad smile never left Cheryl's face! It was one of those precious heavenly gifts that lifted our spirits, and that day looking at the photograph Paul remembered it and said: "I'll never forget it Mummy – the night Cheryl smiled!"

Paul swung back into his busy weekly programme as an eight year old. School and friends, along with gymnastics, B.B., and music lessons filled his days. There wasn't much time to grieve, although he undoubtedly missed his sister. And coming home to Joy helped to fill the gap left by Cheryl. He would fuss over her, read to her, and tickle her incessantly!

As a child Paul was never really interested in having pets, but he did have goldfish. There were always two of them swimming around in the bowl in his room. What he didn't know for a long time, however, was the number of times that he returned home from school to a 'replacement'. Goldfish don't live very long, and so if one died, or was near to it, we would get one to replace it while Paul was out at school! He usually didn't notice, and so for a long time we avoided him having to deal with 'a floating fish situation'! Until one day, a month after Cheryl died, I noticed that 'Spock' looked a bit 'off'. But then I promptly forgot about it.

Paul arrived home from school as chirpy as ever, and went upstairs to change. Within a few minutes the sound of wailing could be heard. "Oh no," I thought, "the goldfish ... I forgot about the goldfish!" I ran into the hall to see our distressed son standing at the top of the stairs, goldfish bowl in hand. "It's not fair, Mummy!" he sobbed. "My goldfish and my sister are dead! What am I going to do? Why did my goldfish have to die too?"

I ran upstairs to comfort him (*and* to prevent him from dropping the bowl, whose water was splashing all over the floor with his shaking!). His reaction to the dead fish was way out of proportion – but experiencing *another* loss was simply too much for him to bear. It took a long time to settle him, and I'm sure the distress was really more about his sister than his goldfish.

However one lovely thing about grief in young children is that they seem to have the ability to move through it more quickly than adults. One summer's day, six months later, we were returning from a visit to the cemetery, and I could see Paul in the rear-view mirror. He was unusually quiet, and so I asked him what was wrong. "I've got something to tell you, Mummy," he said, "but I don't want it to make you sad." "That's okay, Paul," I replied, rather puzzled, "just tell me anyway." "I've decided not to be sad, anymore, about Cheryl," he remarked, while changing his position to watch my reaction. "Oh!" I said, rather surprised. "And why is that?" I asked, while trying to keep my eyes on the road. "I'm not going to be sad because Cheryl is in Heaven, and she won't have to be sick *ever again*! And I'm glad about that!" "You're not cross with me, are you, Mummy?"

I could see his troubled eyes in the mirror. He genuinely didn't want to hurt me, yet he had worked out in his young heart that Heaven *was* better for Cheryl, and so it was really quite logical – he wouldn't be sad any more! And my heart melted.

Eight
Living Again

JANUARY came, as January does, with short dark days and heavily-laden skies. Staying-at-home weather suited me perfectly, when at least the sunshine wasn't around to mock my mood. I went out when it was expected of me, but the winter months gave me a more natural opportunity to hide away from people whenever possible.

As I watched Paul return to school after the Christmas break, I envied him somewhat. A child's ability not to dwell on anything for too long was a trait I greatly desired, as the depth of my sadness was relentless. Joy had also returned to school, having recovered from her bout of flu. Filling the hours was not easy for me, as my decision making was poor. Often even the simplest of tasks would take a long time to perform, or be left undone. Visitors were also treated with a mixture of responses – either welcome relief or reluctant endurance.

As expected, the number of visitors decreased after the funeral, but we were still well cared for by our large group of friends and church family. Professional visitors continued to call to see Joy, but I had a sneaking suspicion their visits were to check on how I was doing as well. One day a member of the Children's Hospital bereavement team arrived for a visit, and as I looked at the young woman sitting across the room from me, I both admired and was puzzled by her. Her job on the hospital's social work team was to counsel families who had a child die at the hospital. I couldn't think of a more distressing form of employment than visiting families in the early stages of grief! She, however, seemed relaxed, thoughtful, and was obviously very good at her job.

She listened. In fact she said nothing at all for a long time, letting me tell her about Cheryl and how she had died. I appreciated the opportunity given to talk to someone who wasn't close, and therefore, who couldn't be hurt by what I said. At the same time it was strange to talk about Cheryl with someone who had never met her. There was, however, one thing she said to me that didn't make sense at the time, but which I have proved down through the years to be absolutely true. "Catherine," she said, "your life will never be the same again – *but it doesn't have to be worse!*" She went on to say that it *is* possible to live again after the death of a child, but that it would take a lot of readjustment: "One day, you won't feel as bad as you do today, and that will be the start of planning for the future again." "Future! What future?" was my silent retort.

Talk of support groups and further counselling just didn't grab me – I was already surrounded by lots of people who provided me with all I needed. That is, apart from one thing . . . Cheryl!

Whenever I could summon up either the energy or the motivation, my days were filled with plenty to keep me busy. I had a bright, bubbly eight year old son, and a darling daughter, of four, who required my attention 'twenty-four seven'. Having Joy meant that my connection with the same doctors, therapists and teacher was unbroken, and there was a certain comfort in maintaining that contact. Unfortunately I was finding no pleasure in anything I did; even nursing Joy just made me want Cheryl more. My heart was empty, yet at the same time it felt like a lead weight. Fake smiles became the mask I hid behind, and as the world moved on, I wanted to go back – back to the days when Cheryl was there at every turn.

Grief, I discovered, is cruel and illogical. "Sure, you have two other children who need you," some folk would say. But the child I longed for most at that time, was the one who didn't need me anymore. Grief is also very lonely, and selfish. It condemns you to solitary confinement – makes you feel as if no one else is suffering like you, even though there are others who are grieving too. Yet you just can't see it! I found grief to be like a great big coat that you pick up everyday, and choose to wear, not daring to dispose of it, in case the one you are grieving for might think you don't care any more. Grief becomes your hiding place, but it doesn't keep you safe, because it seems to shut the door on hope! And, worst of all, grief becomes your accuser, as it is fertile ground in which feelings of guilt can flourish.

Guilt dogged my footsteps. "If only I hadn't left her that night!" I would repeat to myself over and over again. "If only I had gone back to the ward, after Philip returned home!" "How could I have left her alone to die?" was the accusing question that became the belt that fastened the coat of grief tighter around me.

Yet from the depths of my soul came a whisper that I chose to ignore … "She was not alone, Catherine, *I* was with her – just as I promised you I would be." The distant voice of God was held at bay by my distress, and anger. Anger that He had not allowed me to be with my child when I felt she needed me the most … anger at the thought of caring for her for ten long years, only to be denied those last precious moments with her. But anger directed at God is not only sinful, it also destructive.

For the previous ten years I had experienced the love and support of the God of Heaven. Often He had turned my despair into hope … my disappointment into peace … my sorrow into joy. There had been special times when His presence was so real, I was sure that if I had stretched out my hand, I could have touched Him. Now I kept at a distance the only One who could: "Give the oil of joy for mourning, and the garment of praise for the spirit of heaviness." (Isaiah 61:3)

Instead, I tried to assuage my guilt, and comfort my soul by attempting to be as close to Cheryl as I thought I could be. So every day I drove the twenty minute journey to visit her grave; while each Saturday night I would sit by her empty bed trying to make up for the Saturday night I had left her alone to die. And still I had no peace. Instead I allowed grief and guilt to do the work of the enemy of my soul – to torment and accuse me.

And so the months rolled on with very few people aware of the awful devastation that was wreaking havoc in my life. I had become an accomplished actor, putting on a good front, and accepting the readjustments that had to be made - with good effect. After all, my husband was a preacher, and it wouldn't do to let people see how the preacher's wife had all but crumbled on the inside! "Isn't it better for her," folk would remark. "And it takes the burden from you as well," they would add, assuming that Cheryl's death was some kind of relief for us. My response would be a false smile, but inwardly I would be saying: "Why should the death of my child be any different from another?" I questioned silently. "Just because she was handicapped, doesn't mean we miss her any less than a 'normal' child!"

Joy's fifth birthday came in July, six days before what would have been Cheryl's eleventh. All the family gathered for the party, only this time Paul had just one set of candles to blow out! He had decorated the room with hand-painted banners, and struck up 'Happy Birthday' on his keyboard when I carried her downstairs earlier that morning. But I could see that his effort was about more than Joy's birthday – he wanted a happy Mummy too! And I tried very hard to be all things to all people, but the sadness refused to lighten, and God appeared to be silent.

We were careering towards Cheryl's first anniversary, and all I could think about was how wrong that social worker had been. Life *was* worse since Cheryl died – it could *never* be the same again! For ten years so much of my life had been bound up in that child. My days were organized by caring for her – even my spiritual life was greatly affected by her. I had learnt so much about God because of her. His word had taken on a new dimension in my life during those years. I relished the time I spent in His presence, and enjoyed the company of God in a way I had not previously experienced. And I believed it was all because of Cheryl! For eight years I had even crossed the country speaking at ladies' meetings, encouraging women to trust God with the most difficult circumstances of their lives.

But since she left me, I felt spiritually bereft. In a strange way I was equating my relationship with God to Cheryl alone. And now she was gone, I didn't seem to have any reason left to live. I was never suicidal - I just felt that I would never *truly* live again, now that she was gone. As far as I could see there could be no happiness, no fulfilment, no purpose left in my life without her.

I was convinced that I should learn to accept this form of existence, while at the same time I knew deep down that God was working on my behalf. Even in this 'dark night of the soul', I realized that the answer to my need was in giving up my anger, and trusting in the One who had never let me down before.

So I returned to prayer – not the 'God bless the whole world' type of praying that I had been fooling myself with, believing that I was okay spiritually because I managed a few verses of the bible, and a few words with God before I closed my eyes at night. No, I returned to honest communication with my Saviour. No more trying to fool Him, (as if I could!). I simply told Him how I felt – the anger, the bitterness, the intense sadness and the feelings of hopelessness all spilled out of my broken heart.

I knew He would know what to do with it all – and with the honesty came a glimmer of a rift breaking through the dark clouds that were my daily companions. Genuine smiles started to cross my face. Real enjoyment with my children began to permeate my days. The weight in my chest seemed very slightly lighter, and the whispers of God were remaining for longer, as I repented of my anger toward Him.

And everyday the request of my heart was always the same: "Please God, show me if there is any reason left for me to live?"

God's response came one quiet Sunday afternoon. Philip was out, Paul was at Sunday school, and Joy was having her afternoon nap. I always loved Sunday, as we had made it our practice to honour the Sabbath by keeping it special. It was not out of legalism, but out of a genuine love for the Saviour that we decided early in our marriage, to make Sunday different. Watching television, shopping and the like were kept for other days, while we aimed Sunday's activities at worshipping the One who had given His *all* for us. It has never been a chore; rather, it has been a delight, and particularly on that Sunday, almost a year after Cheryl's passing.

As Joy slept on the settee, I had put a music tape in the hi-fi and started to read, while it quietly played in the background. I closed my bible, and I prayed as I had on so many other occasions before. My prayers were very selfish, so full of 'me', and as I finished, my heart's cry once again was: "God, please show me if there is any reason left for me to live?"

The tape had continued to play while I was praying, and as I blew my nose, and dried my eyes, I could hear God's very clear reply to the incessant questioning of my heart. A young woman, who had been crippled in a diving accident, was singing:

> "I'VE FINALLY FOUND THE REASON FOR LIVING,
> IT'S IN GIVING EVERY PART OF MY HEART TO HIM,
> AND ALL THAT I DO, EVERY WORD THAT I SAY,
> I'LL BE GIVING IT ALL BACK TO HIM ...
>
> FOR...
> WE WERE THE REASON THAT HE GAVE HIS LIFE,
> WE WERE THE REASON THAT HE SUFFERED AND DIED,
> TO A WORLD THAT WAS LOST, HE GAVE ALL HE COULD GIVE,
> TO SHOW US THE REASON TO LIVE ...
>
> *HE* IS MY REASON TO LIVE."

As the song finished I sat dumbfounded at the direct answer to my direct question – and God continued to speak clearly to this seeking, grief-stricken mother. "Catherine," He said, as the music faded, "to be a good wife and mother is right and proper, but it is not to be your reason to live – I am your reason to live." And I was taken back to the cross, where ... "To a world that was lost, Jesus gave all He could give ... to show us the reason to live." And I knew in that instant, as I pictured Him suffering on that Roman cross for me - that *He* was to be my reason to live!

In this world of constant change – God does not change! In this world of suffering – only God can bring true peace! In this world, where people

' We are the reason' written by Gary Valenciano.

cause us disappointment – God is our fulfilment! In this world, where promises are easily broken – only God will *always* keep His! In a world where those we love may leave us – only God will stay with us forever!

There is no doubt that, because of Cheryl, I had walked with God in ways I never thought possible ... but Cheryl's death didn't mean that I was prevented from walking with God again.

In that room I had a choice to make – God had shown me that there *was* a reason left for me to live – and that reason was Him. Was I going to choose to live for Him, or was I going to choose to wrap my coat of grief closer around me and stay in the darkness? At this point, I knew it was up to me. "Pain is inevitable, but misery is optional," is a Barbara Johnston quote that I had used many times when addressing women. Now it was my turn to 'practice what I preached'! Was I going to choose misery, over a renewed walk with the One who could have me stand under the rainbow again? I reminded myself that God had never promised me a life without pain – only His presence in it, so I slipped from the chair to my knees ... and *made Him my reason to live*!

The quietness of that special moment with God was suddenly interrupted with happy chatter, as Philip and Paul returned home. Paul ran to me, but stopped on seeing the red nose and swollen eyes he had seen so many times before. "Are you sad, Mummy?" he questioned, as he threw his arms around me for a tight squeeze. "No Paul, I'm not," I replied honestly. "Mummy is happier than she has been for a long time!" "Yeah!" he shouted, "I'm so glad, Mummy, 'cause I don't like to see you sad."

***

"The Valley of the shadow of death" referred to in Psalm 23 was a place we were meant to "walk through", but I had pitched my tent in it! As I started living again, I was helped out of my valley by an unseen hand. I was soon to discover that I could weep without feeling despair. Sadness was no longer accompanied by hopelessness – but instead by the knowledge that "we don't sorrow as others who have no hope." (1 Thess.4:13) I determined, with God's help, not to allow guilt to spoil the promise that one day I would see my lovely daughter again. The 'missing you' days still rolled over my life with regularity, but never again was I to experience the absolute devastation of the previous year.

Jesus became my ultimate focus – my reason to live. I knew I could trust Him with today, tomorrow, and every other day after that – as long as I kept my eyes fixed on Him. Once more the sun started to shine, breaking up the dark clouds, and revealing the rainbow!

I thought about Cheryl every single day, but there were now some days when I could remember her without pain. I started to look forward to going out for lunch with friends – no longer afraid of whom we might meet, or what they might say. Visiting Joy in the same classroom that she had once shared with Cheryl became enjoyable again – rather than one more place where Cheryl was missing. Joining in games and outings with Paul and Philip brought fun into my life once more ('fun', being a word I didn't think I would ever use again).

The following summer, when Paul was ten years old, we even crossed the Atlantic for the first time! We had an amazing holiday in Canada for three whole weeks, while Joy stayed at home, being spoilt by Granny and Granda. The funny thing about that holiday was that by the end of it, Joy had more of a suntan than we did, as Canada experienced its worst summer weather on record!! Still, the memories we gained were far better than the weather!

And I started to believe that what the social worker had said was actually true: "My life would never be the same again – but it didn't have to be worse!"

Nine
A Special Place

I WAS sorry when the Department of Education decided to leave the word 'Special' out of the names of schools for children with severe learning difficulties. They really are special places, and different from the normal establishments we would know as school. This type of school does not merely facilitate academic learning, but rather it meets a variety of differing needs represented in their pupils.

For children like Cheryl and Joy, a high staff/pupil ratio is provided because of the amount of personal care that is required. The children in the 'special unit' need to be fed and changed – cuddled and comforted, as well as having a tailored programme of 'education', which some educationalists may not even regard as worthy of the name. Sensory stimulation is a widely used tool to encourage response from the children, which in turn receives praise equal to any prize-day tribute for exam success! For parents like us, a smile from our child at the appropriate time can mean as much as any A*!

The class size is kept very small, accommodating 5-7 children with profound disabilities. As the staff work, hands on, for long periods of time with these extremely dependant children, the children become more than mere pupils. It is natural, therefore, that the staff forge strong, affectionate links with the children, and often their families as well. Next to the child's family, the teacher probably spends more time with the child than anyone else during their lifetime.

That fact only hit me after Cheryl had died. As a grieving mother, it was easy for me to forget that there were other important people in my child's life – all of whom had lavished a substantial amount of time, effort, and even love on my child. They too had watched a brave child struggle, and suffer – all the while developing a close relationship with her over the years. And then when that child dies, they also feel the loss very keenly. I became aware of this because Joy was taught by the same teacher as Cheryl, which meant my contact with her remained unbroken.

As I visited the school, I saw how much Lillian Hill, and her staff, missed my daughter. They were very professional, of course, as they tried not to upset me by their comments, yet it was obvious that they, too, enjoyed the opportunity to indulge in reminiscing. Looking around that class of beautiful children, I knew Cheryl would not be the only one that they would have to say goodbye to. I felt enormous gratitude toward Lillian, who was the only member of staff who stayed year-on-year with this special class: gratitude for her commitment, as teaching these children was more than a job to her, and gratitude that she allowed herself to love each of the children in her care – even though it would prove costly. Within about a year of Cheryl's death, Lillian lost another one of her young pupils.

Then early in 1993, the parents of her pupils received an invitation to her home to have a meeting with her husband, Tom, to discuss our views on a children's hospice. Even as a nurse, I had never heard of a hospice for children before. The term 'hospice' conjured up thoughts of cancer, and death – certainly nothing that I felt was relevant to our children. In addition, I knew that the cancer unit in the Children's Hospital already gave remarkable care to children with cancer, and also to their families. However, because I held Lillian in such respect, I decided to go and see what it was all about, while Philip stayed at home that evening to look after Joy.

I don't remember having met Tom Hill before that night. First impressions were of a man who appeared a little nervous, which is no wonder really, since he was surrounded by a group mostly of women, who were already acquainted with each other to some degree. He was very welcoming towards us, making us feel at home in his large sitting room. His quiet, gentle demeanour portrayed a non-threatening manner as he started to explain why he had asked us to come. After talking about how he had watched his wife grieve for Cheryl, and then for Peter, he found himself asking the question: "If Lillian feels this way, how on earth must the families feel?"

He continued, by explaining how he had always loved hearing about this group of children, and how he had started to nip into the classroom to meet them. As he did so, he began to realize all that was involved in their care on a daily basis. "Soon I found myself asking Lillian more and more about what help was available for these families," he went on to say. "Who looks after the children when Mum is sick? How do they manage to get away on holiday? What about the other children in the family?" "Here was a man who was asking all the right questions," I thought, as I listened to him express genuine concern for families with whom he had no personal connection. A rare quality indeed! In a very short time Tom had won over his listeners by his understanding heart, added to which, we also had something in common - for Tom and Lillian had a son of their own with disabilities.

At that time Tom was the administrative director of the N.I. Hospice, which was a facility providing care for terminally ill adults. As we sipped tea, he told us of a recent trip that he had just undertaken to England involving his work, where an opportunity was given for the delegates to visit a children's hospice. His eyes lit up as he told us of his surprise to discover that the place was full of children - just like those in Lillian's class! After that informative visit on providing care for 'life-limited' children he was a driven man - driven by the thought that a much better service could be provided for the 'Joys' and 'Jonathans' of this world!

The words 'life-limited' rested uneasily in my heart. Cheryl's death had forced me to recognize that one day Joy would also die, but some of these parents had probably never thought of *their* child as being included in that scenario – at least not until now! There was no doubt that respite care was all but impossible to obtain for some of our children who required tube feeding, and the like – no doubt that our area had NO paediatric community nursing service at all – and no doubt that there was no provision for any of our children to die at home, whenever the time came. But the thought of looking after our children in a hospice, was still something hard to understand ... that is, until, Tom showed us the video!

On the television screen we were taken to a beautiful place that looked more like a big home than a hospital. The staff wore ordinary clothes, and the bedrooms had adjoining rooms for family members. There was a huge table in the open-plan kitchen, where everyone - children, and parents and staff, met together at meal times as one big family. Parents spoke of how the hospice had supported all of their family, including siblings and grandparents. Staff explained simply that a children's hospice provided care for children who had conditions which would probably prevent them reaching adulthood – hence the term 'life-limited'. The service provided the elusive respite that could keep carers sane, and home visits for support and advice in between stays. But the part that interested me most was that they gave families the choice of where their children would spend their last days. For us there was no choice – our children would die in hospital, because there was no support available for those of us who wanted our child to die in the familiar surroundings of home, or in a peaceful hospice.

We all watched in silence for the twelve or so minutes it took to watch the tape. What we were looking at was revolutionary! It was hope generating. It showed us the kind of place we thought existed only in our dreams. Everything Tom had said before was clearly brought into focus. A children's hospice was a place where children and their families could get on with living, for whatever time they had, and a place that could help them with the dying.

Before I could speak, someone else had said what was on all our minds: "Can we not have one of these hospices for our children?" Tom's delight at our positive response was obvious, as we all tried to speak our approval at the same time. "It will take time to make a proper case to present to the Hospice Council," he interrupted. "We will have to prove the need for a children's hospice here in Northern Ireland – it will involve a lot of work and effort, but if you give me your support I'm willing to try." All of that small group of parents had been used to hard work, and to fighting for our children - often against the odds, so there and then we asked Tom Hill to start the process, and we would back him to the hilt!

None of us realized in 1993 how long it would take to realize those dreams. The Council quickly dismissed the first approach Tom made, requesting consideration of a service for life-limited children. But Tom Hill was a visionary – a dream maker, and a risk-taker. As he gathered more and more information about the growing children's hospice movement, he was encouraged to persevere. Added to which, there were a number of little faces etched on his mind that kept him going when lesser men might have given up!

So month after month, he added the case for a children's hospice to the agenda, slowly wearing down the resistance of those who felt that they had enough to do running an adult service. And at last a sub-committee was formed to look at Tom's proposal, and provide more information for the Hospice Council. The first hurdle had been crossed, and the families were delighted! Meetings with relevant children's professionals were set up to discuss the current poor provision for life-limited children in the Province. We, along with other parents, told our personal stories of yawning gaps in service provision, but none of these cash-strapped authorities were prepared to initiate the changes that were needed. Instead they were only too glad that a voluntary organization might do their job for them!

Facts from paediatricians and GPs helped bolster our case with facts, and the sub-committee was eventually won over. In 1997 it was my privilege to accompany them, on behalf of the families, to a visit to Acorns – a children's hospice in Birmingham. What an amazing day that was! Then on our return, the sub-committee recommended (*years* after Tom's initial proposal) the setting up of a Children's Hospice Project to fund the building and running of a Children's Hospice service for Northern Ireland!

By that time Philip and I thought it would be too late for Joy to benefit from such a service, but we threw our weight behind it for all the families who would follow after us. In our view, there was no-one better than Tom Hill to direct the project, and we were delighted when his appointment was made official.

And in the mercy of God, Joy was still alive to attend the official launch of the Project on 28th February, 1998. Sister Francis Dominica, an Anglican nun and founder of the worldwide Children's Hospice Movement launched the Project, and it was our privilege to share the platform with her that day. (Her work at Helen House, in Oxford, remains the Gold Standard for children's hospice care throughout the world.) It was a nerve-wracking, exciting, and proud day, as we were interviewed by reporters from television, radio, and newspaper, all wanting to know about Joy (and her sister before her), and how a hospice would change the lives of families like ours.

And so began a whirlwind year of speaking at events, and representing what the media affectionately termed 'the founding families'. Photographs of Joy, Jonathan, Natasha, Rebecca, Nicole, Ashleigh and Ellen were seen on billboards, newspapers, concert programmes and collecting boxes all over Northern Ireland, as the people of our little province took the children to their hearts, and went into a fund-raising frenzy!

At that time, however, Joy's health was deteriorating, but we continued our involvement, allowing the public at times to see what we would have preferred to keep private. The belief that people needed to know what caring for a life-limited child was *really* all about, sometimes resulted in intrusion, misrepresentation and hurt. But in the majority of cases it resulted in an outpouring of support and love from every corner of our province. People from all backgrounds and persuasions got together to build a children's hospice! Even Prince Charles added his support by meeting with the families at a special event in the Spring/Summer of 1998!

All of the founding families were involved in one way or another. And I pay tribute to them for the personal sacrifices they made in order to see the Children's Hospice become a reality. The project would have floundered were it not for the determination, and willingness of seven families to make public their personal heartache.

As for the children – I take my hat off to all of them. You are special, every one! Thanks go to you Natasha, Ashleigh, and Ellen – and also to the memory of Joy, Jonathan, Rebecca and Nicole; not forgetting Cheryl and Peter, whose deaths had provided the momentum for the whole project. These are the unsung heroes of a service for life-limited children that came into being in 2001, enabling families with a life-limited child to enjoy the provision that exists today.

Sadly, however, as with many noble causes, sin can often spoil what is good. Our dear friend Tom Hill did indeed fulfil his dream, but did so ultimately at great cost to himself, because of the ill-founded actions of others. Our heartfelt thanks go to Tom, without whom there may never have been a Children's Hospice in N. Ireland.

Ten
On Butterfly Wings

IF ever a name suited anyone – Joy's name suited her. She was such a pleasant child. Our photograph albums are a testament to that. While Cheryl lost her smile when she was very young, Joy continued to charm everyone by the one thing that she could do well – smile! Paul loved to read to her from books that had accompanying silly sounds, which without fail brought a smile across her face. She also loved music to be playing around her, even though she was unable to locate where the sound was actually coming from. While her visual response was difficult to assess, it was obvious that she could hear the proverbial grass growing!

But she had absolutely no idea how to distinguish between the differing sounds that she heard. She would react to a stern shout in exactly the same way as she would to a lullaby – she would simply smile. Her startle reflex had left her early on in her development, and very few noises seem to frighten or alarm her – except for one … the sound of a trumpet! Whereas loud noises often made her giggle, the trumpet always caused her lip to drop and tears to come. That greatly distressed Paul, who was playing trumpet from the age of ten! His little sister just couldn't appreciate his gift! Instead he had to stick to playing the piano for her, and make sure the trumpet sounds were kept at a distance!!

So every Christmas and birthday, Joy received gifts of noisy or tactile toys to encourage these responses. From a young age, Paul was into making 'things' that usually included lights of all sizes! He once made Joy an amazing flashing, coloured light box to try to stimulate her sight. We all enjoyed it, even if we were unsure as to how much Joy could actually see of it! Paul loved her, and as her big brother he always made time for her.

Joy's giggling did start to concern me, however, even though the whole family seemed to derive such pleasure from it. She would throw her head back, and out would come a real belly laugh that set everyone within ear-shot into kinks of laughter. The only problem was that we could stop laughing when we wanted to, whereas Joy seemed unable to do so. Sometimes she would giggle herself into exhaustion, by which time no-one else thought it funny! Then about a month after Cheryl died, when Joy was four, the paediatrician had called at our home to see us. A short time into the visit Joy started to giggle. Even the doctor laughed at first, but when it continued I could see the look on the doctor's face change. By the time she left we were told that these giggling fits were simply that – 'fits' of epileptic activity over which Joy had no control.

Like Cheryl, Joy's seizures had started around the age of two, but this type of seizure was completely new to me. We were rather sad that this seemingly funny behaviour was in fact doing Joy's brain harm, and it was difficult to discourage Paul from doing anything that would make her laugh. He really did love making her laugh! Unfortunately this type of seizure was not easy to control, and so yet more medication was added to her daily regime, making her response slightly duller, but thankfully not stopping it altogether!

For the next few years things ticked along rather normally for us, with no major emergencies. However, Joy's problem with writhing muscles was made worse by jerking movements, which could have her off your knee in a flash if you weren't holding on to her tightly! (The condition was described by her paediatrician as choreo-athetosis.) In essence it caused muscles inside the body to move in an un-natural fashion, like those in her limbs. One of the consequences of this was that Joy suffered similar stomach problems to those we had seen years earlier in Cheryl.

She had started to suffer from gastric reflux, which caused her pain, while at the same time she found swallowing difficult. Feeding her took such a long time, and the effort she expended while doing so probably used up all the calories in the dish! She would cough and splutter throughout the whole exercise, and neither of us enjoyed the experience! Input from the speech therapist, physio, and new seating did nothing to help solve the problem. So, when she was eight years old, Joy was admitted to hospital for assessment of her feeding problems.

Thankfully, for all of our sakes, she wasn't admitted to the ward where Cheryl had died. A small twelve-bedded unit, below the main hospital corridor, had been renovated to provide eight paediatric neurology beds, and a four-bedded dermatology ward. It was away from the busy bustle of the hospital, yet was bright and welcoming. But the best bit for me was that I really felt Joy was in the safe hands of staff who had experience in caring for children with complex needs. Our son was even more delighted to discover that the ward carried his name – Paul Ward! In the years to come, the staff became almost like extended family members – and the side-ward was affectionately referred to as Joy's second bedroom!

However, Joy's initial admission to Paul Ward was purely for observation and assessment. She was otherwise healthy, and I had checked that the ward was free of the brochiolitis outbreak that was affecting other parts of the hospital at that time. I was reassured that Joy would not be at risk from this viral chest disease that virtually closed wards annually, and caused severe illness and even death in the very young and vulnerable. So Joy and I passed a rather boring week, with the occasional test being carried out, and various experts coming along and making suggestions to try and resolve her feeding problems.

A cup of tea was always a welcome break in the monotony, and as parents were allowed the use of the ward kitchen outside of the children's mealtimes, it was often there that parents met one another and shared stories of their child's illness, and subsequent progress. I had noticed during the week that the side-ward opposite the area where Joy was being nursed, seemed to be cloaked in secrecy. The door was kept closed, and it was clear that the child inside was very ill. Those visitors who quietly moved in and out looked stressed and weary, at times wearing tear-stained faces. My heart went out to them all, as I knew exactly how they felt. So I prayed, asking God to heal their child.

One evening I was standing alone in the kitchen, waiting for the kettle to come to the boil, when another lady joined me. I recognised her as the mother of the child in the side-ward. The atmosphere was very uncomfortable as we waited for the 'watched kettle', so I decided to break the silence: "I do hope your little one is improving ... I have been praying for him." And my empathy for her broke the dam and her tears flowed. As I put my arm around this stranger's shoulders to try to offer comfort, I sensed the kind of despair that I knew only too well. "You don't need to tell me anything," I quickly added, not wanting to intrude on private ground.

Yet sometimes conversing with a stranger can give you the freedom to say the things that would cause pain to those who are nearest to you. And so as I rattled a spoon in the big mug of tea that I had made for her, she opened her heart to me for a few short minutes. She went on to explain how her, previously healthy, two year old son had succumbed to bronchiolitis two weeks earlier. Her chin wobbled, and huge, hot tears once more brimmed over and rolled down her cheeks, as she related how he appeared to be losing his battle with this dreadful disease. "The doctors don't think he's going to make it," she wept.

We stood together in silence for a few short seconds – two mothers, strangers – yet companions in this journey, seeking health for our children. After she composed herself – we walked the short distance into the ward together. I never saw her again. When I returned to the ward early the next morning, the side-ward was empty.

Fear now took up residence alongside sadness as I thought of that little boy. Over a week earlier we had been told that there was no bronchiolitis in

Paul Ward, yet that was evidently not the case. But for now I decided to keep my concerns to myself.

Feeding Joy that lunchtime was more difficult than usual. She was choking, and spluttering, and all within view of the paediatrician who was providing weekend cover for the ward. When the doctor had finished with the child she had come to see, she approached us with a disturbed look on her face. "Why is . . . *this child* . . . not being tube fed?" she asked as she searched for Joy's name on the sign above her bed. I was rather shocked at her interference, as she wasn't Joy's doctor, but replied that I wanted to keep things as normal as possible for Joy. "I would really prefer not to go down the road of artificial feeding," was my final remark. "I would certainly not call *this* 'normal'!" she said, waving her hand at Joy's poor attempts at swallowing.

As she left the room, I felt humiliated and perplexed. Of course the doctor was right in her assessment of what she had observed - up to a point. "Why did she have to watch you today, Joy?" I moaned. "What's up Honey?" I queried as I lifted her out of her chair. "You're just not yourself this morning." Then as I went to tuck in her clothes, my hands touched her bare back and I gasped: "You are burning up, Joy!"

Five hours later, after X-rays, examinations and physiotherapy to obtain samples from her lungs, Joy was worse. In fact she looked very sick indeed! The ward sister came and sat down beside me with a look that told me all was not well. "Catherine, we will have to move Joy into the side-ward," she said. "The doctors are afraid she may have bronchiolitis!" As she started to prepare for the move I could contain my frustration in no longer: "Why was I told, over a week ago, that there was no bronchiolitis in the ward, when that little boy had it!" Sister knew the excuses she presented were feeble in the light of Joy's condition, and she also realized that what Joy was suffering from was hospital acquired!

To make matters worse, when the 'on call' paediatrician returned, she requested that we allow Joy to be tube fed, as she no longer had the energy required to feed by mouth. So Joy experienced tubes, and drips and oxygen for the first time – and my heart sank. "Is this where it starts, Lord?" I whispered, as a sense of déjà vu gripped my heart. The next few weeks were nightmarish, as Joy's condition deteriorated because she was exposed to yet another, but more serious, hospital acquired infection. This organism went on to colonize in her lungs, only to flare up at regular intervals and become a most serious cause of lung disease for Joy.

When we eventually left the hospital Joy was in a far worse condition than when she had entered it. We took home a sick, weak child who required fairly intensive nursing; she now needed tube-feeding, inhaled medication, and also suctioning to help keep her lungs clear. Deep down I knew we had stepped on to the 'Roller Coaster' once again, and I wasn't looking forward to the ride.

Paul was now a teenager, and starting to see the unfairness of life more clearly. His little sister stayed quite little, as she continued to lose weight. Her days were often plagued by sickness, but he would tenderly slip her on to his knee and read to her from her 'noisy' books. The smiles came less easily now, but if anyone could draw them from her, it was Paul. We never had any doubt that she recognized Paul's voice. Now and then, all three of us would talk about Heaven, but it was less often than before. Instead Paul became good at sorting out the various pieces of equipment that Joy needed, and making sure his mum was okay, especially when his dad was away preaching.

Joy's difficulties were contrasted by Paul's blossoming musical talent. Music was in his blood (well, on the Campbell side anyway!) and he seemed to excel at everything he put his hand to. Music festivals and school concerts were a great diversion, and we loved the chance to encourage him whenever we could. His teenage years were a breeze, and for that we thank God! Even the staff on Paul Ward loved to catch up with all that he was doing, when he came to visit Joy during her many admissions.

***

Whereas Cheryl's last few years had been, for the most part, spent quietly sleeping, Joy's were dreadful. She slept only for very short periods, and appeared to be in a lot of pain. In time the vomiting problem was making her life a misery, with fears that it could also be adding to her breathing difficulties. So in 1997, after much discussion, we reluctantly agreed to gastric surgery, in order, "To give Joy some quality of life, for whatever time she had left," as the surgeon had put it.

Sitting in the ward, we became anxious as Joy's time in theatre went long past what we were told to expect. Eventually we sighed with relief as we saw the surgeon come toward us, still dressed in his theatre greens. Just as quickly we realized that he wasn't smiling. "It's over!" he said, and we waited for the 'but'. "But … the surgery was much more difficult than I expected," he continued, trying to explain what had happened. "Joy bled a lot in theatre … but we've managed to stop the bleeding. The staff from Intensive Care will send for you when they get her settled."

His look of exhaustion matched our look of anxious disappointment. And a little wave of panic swept over me, as the enemy of my soul teased me with the suggestion that perhaps surgery was the wrong decision after all. Seeing Joy later in ICU did nothing to dispel those doubts, and for Philip it was one of the worst moments of his life!

Joy's recovery was hampered by one complication after another, and I longed day after day to take her home – to escape somehow, and take her away from all this suffering! At times we can equate a place with a problem. For example - Joy was in Paul Ward, and therefore it was the ward's fault that she was so ill – so if I could take her home, then she would be okay!! My thinking was totally illogical – but the staff got to know that the more ill Joy became, the more I wanted to take her home! Eventually both sides came to realize that my problem was that I didn't want Joy's death to be like Cheryl's. I really wanted Joy to die at home. So after discussing it with her paediatrician, I was promised, that if at all possible, I would be able to take Joy home when the time came. It brought some degree of peace.

Early on the 28th July, 1997, I slipped into the ward to discover that I wasn't the only one with secret plans for the day! A silver banner was already attached across the top of the side-ward door, announcing: "Happy Birthday!" to Joy! Inside, two of my 'favourite' nurses were just finishing dressing her in the birthday dress I had left for her the night before. (They had come in early in order to have her ready before I arrived!) Bright ribbons draped her cot, and a little pile of presents and cards were already sitting on the bedcover!

Philip and Paul joined the celebrations soon afterwards, and some of Paul's masterpieces were added to the decorations! All day staff from other departments, who knew Joy, called in to see her, and as family and friends swelled the numbers too, Joy's little side-ward was buzzing with laughter and happy chatter! She was twelve years old that day, just as it said on the big badge that her brother had attached to her dress! And although she didn't get to taste the cake baked for her in the hospital kitchen, all of her visitors did!

At twelve, she wore clothing to fit a five year old, and therefore had remained small enough to be cuddled and held, looking more like a toddler than nearly a teenager! Thankfully, not long after her birthday we were able to take her home once again.

Unfortunately, due to the complications that arose during her surgery, Joy did not regain any improvement in her quality of life. Instead, I felt she had merely exchanged one form of discomfort for another. Her nutrition was now more severely compromised than ever, thereby further lowering her resistance to infection. Early in December, 1997, Joy was back in hospital for what we thought would be her last time. Family and friends rallied with their support and prayers once more, as they had been doing faithfully for our family over a period of some eighteen years!

Watching Joy suffer on a daily basis was difficult for us all. Philip was trying to continue in his ministry as an itinerant evangelist, yet he found it increasingly difficult to be away from home. So he had started to carry a small pager with him to ensure he could be contacted quickly if necessary. Meanwhile Paul was in the middle of studying for his GCSE examinations. I was the one who spent most of the time at the hospital, and I was starting to feel the old pangs of anger and resentment grow again as I watched the precious 'baby' of our family suffer.

"Why does it have to be this way, Lord?" I would question. "It's so unfair!" Yet alternatively, I dreaded becoming bitter and despairing as I had before. So I asked God to set a guard on my heart. "Help me to *choose* acceptance." I would plead. "Help me to trust You with what I can't understand, Lord!" And slowly I began to realize that the darkest time Joy would have to go through would provide her with the brightest of all rainbows – *the promise of Heaven*. That rainbow held the promise of . . . no tears . . . no more pain . . .no sorrow . . . no more death . . . forever! And the ultimate joy . . . God Himself will be with us! (Revelation 21)

And as I held her, especially when she was distressed, I would tell her it would soon be over, and sing to her every song I knew about Heaven! I read about Heaven, and I thought about Heaven, and I sang about Heaven . . . until its very brightness started to break up the blackness of despair.

But Joy *did* survive that Christmas, and although from that time onwards she required oxygen and monitoring, and occasional blood transfusions on top of everything else, I knew she had been spared for a purpose. For it was in February 1998 that the Children's Hospice Project was launched, and Joy (along with other children) helped spearhead that campaign. God had given our brave little girl one more job to do before allowing her to stand under her final rainbow!

***

"I've got her bedroom ready for her, Catherine," the staff nurse said over the phone. "The paediatrician told us you were on your way – so just come on in as soon as you can." As we drove to the hospital I reckoned that almost fifteen months had passed since that dreadful Christmas when we were expecting Joy to leave us. She was now a teenager - a thought I didn't like, because the term almost mocked the slip of a little girl that she was. Spring was just around the corner, and the days had started to stretch. Hope was on its way for another year, another season when life would shoot from the earth once more.

But Joy had become very ill once again. This time her bowel had stopped working, which had led to a small part of her lower left lung collapsing. It was down to waiting time again. It had been explained to us a short time before, that Joy's organs were starting to 'give up', as she had now entered what was referred to medically as 'the terminal phase' of her condition.

A few days later it was Mothers' Day (14th March 1999), and Philip was to come and relieve me at the ward while I went to speak at a Ladies' church service on behalf of the Children's Hospice Appeal. I lifted Joy out of her cot to dress her, but her breathing became distressed as I tried to do so, and, feeling that I couldn't leave her, I sent Philip to the service instead! By the time he had returned to the ward, I had made up my mind that it was time to bring Joy home. Philip agreed – there was nothing more anybody could do for Joy, and we wanted her be home with all the family. We decided that we would talk to Paul about it later, and ask the doctor for permission to take Joy home the next day.

Chest physiotherapy can appear quite brutal sometimes, and Paul arrived with his granny just as the physio (whom we knew very well) was doing her 'stuff'. Joy rarely got upset with this procedure, as she was so used to it, but on this occasion a slight moan was heard as her chest was pummelled. Paul, now seventeen, seemed to sense right away that Joy was very unwell, and as he watched, he suddenly caught the physio's arm and shouted at her: "Why don't you leave her alone!" he yelled. "Can't you see that you're hurting her?" "Paul!" I exclaimed, startled at this unusual outburst from him. With that he ran out of the room, with Granny in close pursuit. "Let him be, Catherine," said the physio, as I tried to apologize. "He's just upset," she remarked, with an understanding look. "He can see how sick Joy is, and he's only trying to protect her."

Reassurance, rather than rebuke was what was needed as I realized that the physio's comments were correct. Paul was anxious and embarrassed, and trying to cover it up he took out a parcel and placed it under Joy's arm: "Happy Mother's Day, Mum – from both of us!" With hugs and jokes we tried to lighten the atmosphere, and I then got the chance to kiss my own mother, thanking her for loving all of us! Joy was too weak to be held, and dozed off after an exhausting afternoon.

Soon the room was quiet again, and I sat for a few minutes enjoying the silence. Then I walked down to the ward kitchen and filled the kettle. It was a slow old thing, so I came back to fetch the dish of pasta my mum had brought up for my tea. "Time you went over on your side, Sweetheart," I said to the still sleeping Joy, as I slid my arms under her and turned her from her back to rest on her right side.

Almost immediately the alarm on the oxygen measuring monitor went off, creating a loud noise. I looked to see if I had knocked off the probe when I had turned her over – no, it was still in situ. Glancing at Joy I could see that she was struggling to breathe. Immediately I reached for the oxygen valve and turned it up, quickly returning her to her previous position on her back. The alarm was displaying a very low level of oxygen saturation in her blood. Her breathing was fast, her lips grey, and the alarm was still screaming! "Why have none of the girls come? Can't they hear the noise!" I ran out of the room shouting: "Nurse!" Immediately they sprang into action – one going for a doctor, while the other worked with the oxygen and Joy, trying to get both into harmony again.

After about ten minutes the crisis was over – Joy's oxygen level had improved, but she groaned pathetically when the doctor was listening to her chest. "Poor Joy," the doctor said to her, "you are having a bad day! We'll just take a picture of your chest and see what's going on." I loved it when the medics spoke to Joy personally. I knew the comments were really for me, but I liked it when they treated her as a little individual, in her own right.

The pasta had been 'zapped' in the microwave, and I had just settled down to eat it when the doctor returned with the X-ray. She held it against the light, and pointed to one side of it. "It's not good," she said with a deep sigh. "The rest of Joy's left lung has collapsed, and she's only working on one lung now." I didn't flinch, as my protection mechanism went into operation. No tears, no panic – nothing! I felt nothing – I said nothing! She cleared her throat, as she went on to say: "I've spoken to the 'on call' consultant – he says if you want to take Joy home, you can." Still I didn't speak. I just reached forward and held Joy's hand, while an inner voice said: "I will be with you."

My mind was in a whirl, and the doctor sounded like she was in the distance now, but I could just about hear her say: "If her oxygen level drops again, it's unlikely she will survive – do you understand what I am saying?"

She seemed to sense that I wasn't quite with her. "I've heard it all before," I replied, in a manner that must have sounded a bit rude, as I tried to decide whether things really were that bad.

"Catherine, Joy has never been this ill before – I don't think she'll see the morning." With that she turned to go. "I'm sorry," I said, stopping her for a few short seconds, as quiet tears at last started to fall, "I'll speak to my husband about taking Joy home – we would really like that."

***

By ten o'clock that night Joy was tucked up snugly in bed in her own room at home. Unfortunately, we had very little time to prepare Paul for the sudden decision that was forced on us because of Joy's deterioration. When we arrived home he was agitated and confused. "Why have you done this, Mum? If Joy is so ill, why have you brought her home?" he questioned, as he sat on her bedroom floor while I was sorting things out. I sensed that somehow he thought this was some mad scheme that his mother had dreamt up, and that because of it we were putting Joy in danger. Stopping what I was doing, I sat on the bed facing Paul, who was clearly hurting. "Son, Joy is *dying* . . . the doctor has said she can either die in hospital or die at home with us . . . which do you think is better for Joy . . . and for all of us?" It was an awful question for a seventeen year old to contemplate – I pulled him off the floor as he sat in silence, with his lip quivering - and I held him close. As my grip relaxed he pulled back and gently replied: "Here, of course . . . but it's not fair, Mummy . . . none of this is fair!"

Amazingly Joy was not only very settled in her own bed, but her oxygen level and pulse had all returned to normal levels! It confirmed to me that we had done the right thing in bringing her home, as I watched her sleeping peacefully under the dim light of the bedside lamp. And because she was so settled, and our bedroom was literally only feet away, we stretched out and dosed lightly, checking her frequently throughout the night.

Suddenly, shortly before 5am, the alarm from the oxygen monitor squealed at us from her room, and we both raced in to see the figures slowly falling. I tried to waken Joy, without wanting to frighten her, while Philip changed the oxygen cylinder that was registering low. His hands shook as he tried to hurry the process, but turning up the new cylinder to a higher rate made no difference. It was happening … the moment we were all dreading – Joy was dying!

"Quickly Philip!" I shouted, "Go and phone our parents – maybe they'll get here in time!" As he ran to the phone, I rushed into Paul's room. He was just stirring with all the noise, and as calmly as I could, I told him that Joy was going fast. "It's up to you, Son, if you want to be with her, you need to come now – if you don't we'll come and tell you when it's over. The choice is yours – I can't make it for you." I felt so guilty as I left his room – guilty that I had caused him so much pain – guilty that he had to make choices that he would have to live with the rest of his life. "Oh God, please give us the grace to get through this!" I cried from my heart.

As I sat at the top of Joy's bed with my arm around her shoulder, Philip sat further down the bed holding her hand. Soon Paul joined us, and reached forward to turn the sound off on the monitor. He sat on the floor in silence. There was a strange sense of peace in the room – God was fulfilling His promise once more, because each of us knew that He was there with us. There was no panic – only silent tears, as we talked to Joy of the lovely place she was going to.

"Don't be afraid, Sweetheart," I said, as I gently planted a kiss on her forehead, and when I lifted my head again, the light from the lamp was shining through the silk butterfly that was clipped to it. In a flash, God gave me a beautiful picture of what was happening to our daughter at that very moment! Just as the butterfly breaks through its chrysalis, leaving its old earth-bound shell behind to soar into the sky, so Joy was leaving behind her old, twisted and pain-filled body to take on her new Heavenly body, which would allow *her* to soar as she had never done before! "Joy," I exclaimed, "look at the butterfly, Pet – you are getting a new body, right now, Sweetheart! Soon you are going to fly … like … the butterfly, straight to Heaven!" She moaned as if distressed, and I told her it was okay to go – that we would be okay.

As the numbers on the monitor plummeted to zero, we each kissed our beautiful, brave Joy goodbye . . . heartbroken at our loss . . . yet heartened by the picture that helped to ease our pain – Joy was now perfect, and for the first time she was soaring!! It was 5am on 15th March, 1999.

***

If a death can ever be described as a 'good' death, then Joy's was. She died at home surrounded by those who loved her, assured that her suffering was over, now with only freedom and perfection ahead. Heartache was undoubtedly revisited – on many occasions . . . but not despair. I had left that at the Cross a number of years earlier, and had also learned since then that peace lies in acceptance - the type of acceptance that rests on the knowledge that God knows what He is doing even when we don't; the type of acceptance that acts on that knowledge and lives each day by faith. That kind of acceptance brings freedom!

Even Joy's funeral was different. Sad – yes, but also triumphant as the large congregation listened to Philip bravely pay his own remarkable tribute to his little girl, as his last act of fatherly love. Paul sat beside me squeezing my hand, as he watched his dad with pride. Later, on that beautiful spring day, they both carried Joy's coffin with the same pride. And the wings of the wildflower butterfly wreath, sitting on her coffin seemed to flutter in the light breeze, reminding me that Joy wasn't earthbound anymore!

Just over a year later, I was standing at the kitchen sink in the manse we had recently moved to in Coleraine, when Paul's little blue car drove into the yard. I smiled as he rushed out of the car, obviously very excited about something! Picking up the towel to dry my hands as he ran through the door, I didn't even get a chance to say "Hello". Instead, he caught me in his arms and twirled me round exclaiming: "Mum you should see it!" "See what?" I replied, rather puzzled. "The Children's Hospice!" he retorted, as if I should have known what he was talking about! "I was driving up the motorway and . . . you should see it Mum . . . the walls are so high now . . . it's amazing!" he

said, hardly stopping for breath. "But you know what's the best bit, Mum –
Joy is in every brick!" And I basked in the pride of the moment.

***

For a period of almost twenty years, God had allowed me to care for our
two beautiful, brave daughters. I have never stopped being their mother – it
is just that we cannot be together for a while. They, however, continue to
bless my life every day that I live. I would be lying if I said that 'I wouldn't
have changed a thing', for what mother would deliberately choose suffering
for her children. What I wouldn't change, however, is the perspective that
having Cheryl and Joy has added to my thinking. I can now value people for
who they are, and not merely for what they can do. And I am utterly
convinced that life here pales into insignificance in comparison to what lies
ahead for those who love Christ. Neither would I want to have missed all that
I have learned about God, and from God. It has been both priceless and
precious!

We are told in the bible that "God is no man's debtor." He doesn't owe
me anything - yet He continues to lavish His goodness upon me. Take Cheryl's
26th birthday for instance – on that day God sent another blue-eyed blonde
into our lives, in the form of Susie – Paul's new bride. God, in His mercy, is
once more allowing me to enjoy the blessings of a 'daughter'!

There is no doubt that many of my days have been storm-filled, but if
they hadn't been, then I wouldn't have got to stand 'Under the Rainbow', and
experience the unfailing promises of God. For that I give God thanks!